10/95

CULTURES OF THE WORLD

DOMINICAN REPUBLIC

Erin Foley

MARSHALL CAVENDISH
New York • London • Sydney

Reference edition published 1995 by
Marshall Cavendish Corporation
2415 Jerusalem Avenue
P.O. Box 587
North Bellmore
New York 11710

© Times Editions Pte Ltd 1995

Originated and designed by
Times Books International, an imprint of
Times Editions Pte Ltd

Printed in Singapore

Library of Congress Cataloging-in-Publication Data:
Foley, Erin.
    Dominican Republic / [Erin L. Foley].
      p. cm.—(Cultures Of The World)
    Includes bibliographical references and index.
    ISBN 1-85435-690-9 (set). — ISBN 1-85435-694-1 :
      1. Dominican Republic—Juvenile literature. [1. Dominican
Republic.] I. Title. II. Series.
F1934.2.F65 1994
972.93—dc20   94–29382
                         CIP
                          AC

Cultures of the World

Editorial Director	Shirley Hew
Managing Editor	Shova Loh
Editors	Elizabeth Berg
	Jacquiline King
	Dinah Lee
	Azra Moiz
	Sue Sismondo
Picture Editor	Susan Jane Manuel
Production	Anthony Chua
Design	Tuck Loong
	Ronn Yeo
	Felicia Wong
	Loo Chuan Ming
Illustrators	Anuar
	Chow Kok Keong
	William Sim
MCC Editorial Director	Evelyn M. Fazio
MCC Production Manager	Janet Castiglioni

INTRODUCTION

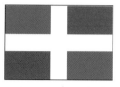

THE DOMINICAN REPUBLIC approaches the end of the 20th century as a democratic nation having survived colonization, foreign invasions, brutal dictatorships, and devastating hurricanes. Although its original inhabitants, the Taínos, were not such fortunate survivors, Dominican culture nonetheless has woven certain elements of the indigenous culture together with the Spanish and African influences that otherwise dominate the society.

In many ways, the Dominican Republic exemplifies Latin America, with its sharp contrasts of extreme wealth and poverty; its vast agricultural regions and noisy, crowded cities; its dry, mountainous regions and lush tropical beaches; and its ancient pre-Columbian artifacts and modern, high-tech industry. The Dominican people themselves are universally known for their cheerful disposition, their love of music and dancing, and a certain resignation in the face of high unemployment and widespread poverty.

CONTENTS

Many rural Dominicans leave for the cities in the hope of finding a better life.

CONTENTS

A dancer shows off the bright colors of a traditional costume, as well as the cheerful friendliness Dominicans are known for.

GEOGRAPHY

THE DOMINICAN REPUBLIC occupies the eastern two-thirds of the island of Hispaniola, one of the principal islands in the West Indian archipelago. A former colony of Spain, it shares the island with Haiti, a Creole French-speaking country that occupies the west end of the island. Hispaniola is located between Cuba to the northwest and Puerto Rico to the east. After Cuba, it is the largest island in the West Indian archipelago.

The Dominican Republic is the second largest country in the Caribbean. It includes 977 miles of coastline, with the Atlantic Ocean to the north, the Caribbean Sea to the South, and the Mona Passage between the eastern tip of the Dominican Republic and Puerto Rico.

Explorer Christopher Columbus described the island of Hispaniola as "the fairest ever looked on by human eyes." It includes steep mountain ranges, semiarid deserts, rich farmlands, lush tropical rainforests, picturesque beaches, and even a saltwater lake.

The original inhabitants, the Taínos, called the island Haiti, but referred to the eastern part of the island as Quisqueya. Dominicans often adopt in popular usage the romantic title of Quisqueya for their country.

Opposite: **With more than 20 distinct geographical regions within an area of approximately 18,657 square miles, the Dominican Republic is one of the most geographically diverse countries in the world.**

Left: **Beef cattle are raised on medium to large ranches in the east.**

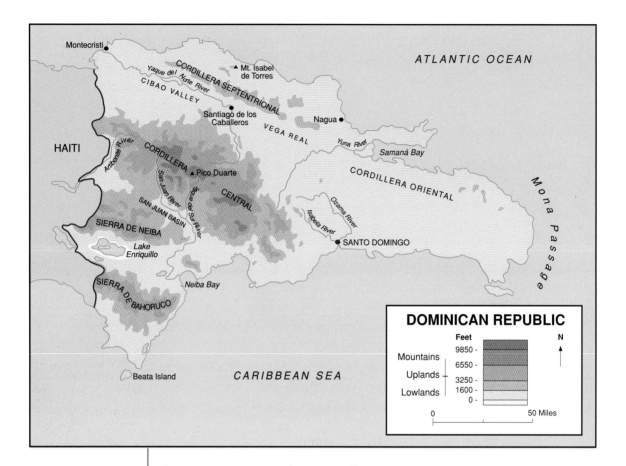

REGIONS

Four mountain ranges divide the country into northern, central, and southwest regions. The Cordillera Central forms the backbone of the country, with smaller but still impressive mountain ranges on either side.

THE NORTHERN REGION The Atlantic coastal plain extends from the northwest city of Montecristi to the city of Nagua. The Cordillera Septentrional ("cor-dee-YEH-rah sep-tent-ree-ohn-AL") rises from the coastal plain in moderate peaks no more than 3,300 feet in elevation.

The rich farmland of the Cibao ("see-BAH-oh") Valley lies below the southern slopes of the Cordillera Septentrional. The Dominican Republic's "second city," Santiago de los Caballeros, presides over the Cibao Valley.

The Cordillera Central can be traced from Cuba, under the Windward Passage to Hispaniola, and again through the Mona Passage to Puerto Rico, where it also forms the Cordillera Central of that island.

To the east of Santiago the Cibao is called the Vega Real, or Royal Plain. The Vega Real is a flood plain with rich, deep topsoil, planted with grains and tobacco.

THE CENTRAL REGION The Cordillera Central, or the Central Range, forms the backbone of the central region. The Cordillera Central crosses the Dominican Republic and Haiti, rising to 10,414 feet at Pico Duarte , the highest point in the Dominican Republic.

The Caribbean coastal plain features a series of limestone terraces, rising to almost 400 feet near the foothills of the Cordillera Oriental.

The western edge of the central region includes the poor agricultural land of the San Juan Basin.

THE SOUTHWEST REGION The Sierra de Neiba towers over the San Juan Basin to the north and the Neiba Valley, or Hoya de Enriquillo, to the south.

Lying in the western part of the bare and dusty Neiba Valley is Lake Enriquillo. It is the largest lake in the Caribbean islands and, as it once formed part of a strait, is filled with pale blue salt water. Crocodiles inhabit the waters and flamingos can be found nearby.

Banana plantations cover a valley. The Cibao Valley ranges from nine to twenty-eight miles in width, and is irrigated by the Yaque del Norte River.

Palm trees grace the banks of a river near Santo Domingo.

RIVERS

The Yaque del Norte is the most significant river in the Dominican Republic. It is approximately 184 miles long and irrigates a basin area of 2,747 square miles. Broken only by the Tavera Dam, the river rises in the Cordillera Central near Pico Duarte at an elevation of 8,462 feet, crosses the Cibao Valley, and empties into the Atlantic Ocean on the northwest coast, where it forms a delta.

The Yaque del Sur is the most important river on the southern coast. Rising at an elevation of almost 8,900 feet in the southern slopes of the Cordillera Central, it serves a basin area of 1,939 square miles. Its course through the mountains accounts for 75% of its length. It empties into Neiba Bay on the southern coast, where it forms a delta.

Salty Lake Enriquillo has a drainage basin that is approximately 1,200 square miles in area and includes 10 minor river systems. Its northern rivers rise year-round in the Sierra de Neiba. Its southern rivers, however, rise in the Sierra de Bahoruco only after heavy rainfall.

Other rivers include the Artibonite along the Haitian border; the San Juan River, which joins up to the Yaque del Sur; the Ozama and the Isabela in the Caribbean coastal plain; and the Yuna River, which rises in the Cordillera Central and empties into Samaná Bay.

CLIMATE

The Dominican Republic has a generally temperate climate. Trade winds and high elevations keep the average annual temperature close to 77°F. Nonetheless, protected valleys can swelter in temperatures over 100°F, and lows of 32°F are not uncommon in the mountains.

For most of the country, the rainy season lasts from May to November. The dry season is from November through April. Along the north coast, however, the rainy season is from November through January. Rainfall comes in short downpours, followed by clear skies and cooler temperatures.

The Dominican Republic receives an average of 60 inches of rain per year, but this also varies according to the region. Periodic droughts have ruined sugar crops and caused severe water shortages, while some parts of the country experience yearly flooding due to poor drainage.

Hispaniola lies in a "hurricane channel" that brings cyclones, tropical depressions and storms, and hurricanes. When a hurricane hits, about once every two years, winds can rise to 125 miles per hour and rainfall drenches the area. Most strike the southern part of the island, especially along the Hoya de Enriquillo.

Trade winds bring mild temperatures, ranging from 64°F in the cooler mountains to 82°F in the warmer and more humid plains and valleys.

Santo Domingo was devastated by a hurricane in 1930. In 1978, Hurricane David killed thousands of Dominicans and caused over one billion dollars in damages, a disaster from which the country still has not completely recovered.

11

Tropical vegetation flourishes in the eastern mountain region, including tree ferns, bromeliads, lianas, and orchids.

Common to the country's 21 species of lizards is a thin, often colorful strip of skin along the throat that blows up like a balloon when the lizard feels threatened.

FLORA

Due to its diverse geography and tropical climate, the Dominican Republic has over 5,600 plant species. About 36% of these species are native to Hispaniola. The Taíno Indians cultivated many plants that are still common today, including manioc, papaya, tobacco, and various species of pepper. The Taínos also cultivated the *higuero* ("ee-GOOAIR-oh") or calabash tree, which they used to make eating utensils and ceremonial masks.

Also native to Hispaniola are trees such as the Dominican magnolia, the mamón tree, the bija, and the ceiba, or silk-cotton tree. The ceiba tree is enormous and can live up to 300 years. Craggy mangrove trees grow in swampy areas.

The eastern mountain region, with its humid forests, has the most luxuriant vegetation. Mahogany trees thrive in abundance; their hard wood was used to build the first cathedral in the Americas. The higher mountain zones of the Dominican Republic are coniferous and include the creolean pine tree. The deserts and semiarid areas of the southwest are characterized by cactus and agave.

Several varieties of palm trees grow on the beaches, including the coconut palm, which was imported from Africa, and the native royal palm.

Spanish settlers introduced mangos, bananas, cocoa, coffee, and sugarcane. Trees such as the coral tree, the African tulip tree, and the flamboyant or poinciana, were also introduced after the Conquest.

FAUNA

The Dominican Republic is home to 18 species of bats, the bottle-nose dolphin, and the West Indian manatee. The solenodon and a rodent called the hutia are nearly extinct. Discovered in 1907, the solenodon resembles an anteater and subsists on insects. Another native mammal, a mute dog that the Taínos raised for meat, is now extinct.

The Spaniards introduced cows, pigs, donkeys, and horses to Hispaniola, as well as mice, rats, and cats. The mongoose, imported from India, is now a pest.

Reptiles live in abundance, especially frogs, snakes, and lizards. Tree frogs live on palm trees, banana trees, and even telephone poles and are very noisy. The American crocodile, the rhinoceros iguana, and the ricard iguana are all endangered species. Scorpions can be found in the drier areas, especially underneath rocks. Spiders are numerous, including a large, harmless tarantula.

Fish include barracuda, eels, parrotfish, leather jacket, sawfish, Spanish and frigate mackerel, red snapper, grouper, mullet, and sardines. Humpback whales reside in the Samaná Bay from December through March. The beaches and tidepools yield a variety of crabs and snails.

The anthozoans that form the Dominican Republic's coral reefs produce calcium carbonate, which forms the surface of much of the island. The northwest coast and parts of the southern coast have abundant coral reefs that depend on a delicate ecological balance to survive.

The Dominican Republic has over 200 species of birds, including flamingos (below), almost half of which live in an aquatic environment. The Hispaniolan parrot and the perico are now rare.

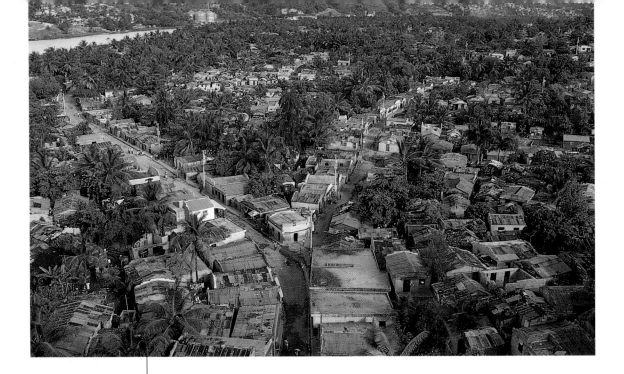

CITIES

SANTO DOMINGO Santo Domingo (population 2.4 million) was established as the first Spanish capital in the Americas. In addition to being the seat of national power and the economic center of the Dominican Republic, it holds the first university, the first cathedral, and the first castle built in the Americas. Many of the colonial attractions are still standing. The "old city" was restored in the 1970s and still has cobblestone streets, open-air markets, and craftsmen working out of small shops. The capital also remains the center of cultural attractions in the Dominican Republic.

More than any other city, Santo Domingo attracts migrants from the countryside and from small towns, and construction rushes to keep up with the influx. Many of the migrants are poor and live in slums inside and outside the city. Santo Domingo is also home to most of the country's growing middle class, whose supermarkets and suburbs cover parts of the city.

SANTIAGO DE LOS CABALLEROS Santiago (population 490,000) is the agricultural center of the Dominican Republic. It has a long tradition of aristocratic families, and it prides itself on being a center of culture and refinement.

LA ROMANA Located on the southern coast, La Romana is a relaxed provincial capital. It has traditionally been the center of the sugar industry, but it is also a popular resort area.

La Romana was long considered a "company town," under the control of a U.S.-based multinational corporation, Gulf and Western. Gulf and Western was one of the largest property owners in the Dominican Republic, investing heavily in sugar refining, cattle, tourism, cement, and real estate. Critics say that the company also often employed brutal administrators who bribed Dominican politicians, local police, and military commanders. To show goodwill, Gulf and Western spent approximately $20 million on the creation of schools, churches, clinics, parks, recreation centers, and employee housing. They sold out their holdings in the 1980s, but La Romana has continued to benefit by and build upon the initial infrastructure.

PUERTO PLATA Originally settled by Christopher Columbus in 1494 as the town of Isabela, Puerto Plata today is the center of the Dominican Republic's hotel and tourist resort boom. The scenic city lies north of Santiago at the foot of Mount Isabel de Torres. It competes with the nation's capital as the largest tourist attraction.

The rapid growth of Puerto Plata, along with investment by companies from the United States, Canada, and Europe, is stimulating the tourist development of surrounding towns.

HISTORY

DOMINICAN HISTORY SURGES with dramatic political and economic struggles for power. The country has been shaped by the influence of its most authoritarian rulers, who in spite of their abuses of power are often admired for their strength and remembered nostalgically for the order and stability that they imposed, however brutally they did so.

The Dominican Republic was forced to fight for its independence not just once but several times. Indeed, the Dominican Republic has throughout its history been subject to the influence of greater powers. It has come under the rule of two European colonial powers, Spain and France, as well as its neighbors, Haiti and the United States.

PRE-COLUMBIAN HISPANIOLA

TAÍNOS When Columbus, or Cristóbal Colón as he is known in Spanish, landed on the island of Hispaniola, he encountered large, permanent settlements of friendly people who referred to themselves as "Taíno" ("tie-EE-no"), meaning "good" or "noble"—evidently to distinguish themselves from the warlike Island Caribs, who were rumored to be cannibals. He called the people "Indians," thinking that he had reached the far eastern edge of Asia.

Modern scholars estimate that the population of Hispaniola numbered about 500,000 inhabitants. The Taíno culture had spread throughout much of the Antilles, but the Taínos of Hispaniola and Puerto Rico were the most populous and the most culturally advanced. The Taínos had no written language.

Opposite: **The Panteón Nacional, established in 1747 as a Jesuit convent, contains the remains of prominent 19th century Spaniards, including General Pedro Santana, who arranged the annexation of the Dominican Republic to Spain in 1861.**

Above: **Christopher Columbus landed on the island of Hispaniola in 1492. He was favorably impressed by the friendliness of the Taínos who greeted him; he was even more impressed by the gold they wore.**

The Taínos employed a sophisticated agricultural system; they heaped up mounds of earth into large regular rows of permanent planting fields, called *conuco* ("koh-NOO-koh"). They cultivated root crops such as sweet potatoes, corn, and most importantly, cassava, which they used to make flour for bread. They also cultivated squash, beans, peppers, and peanuts, which they boiled and ate with meat or fish. In the area around their houses they grew small crops of fruit, calabash, cotton, and tobacco, from which they made cigars. This was the first contact Europeans had with tobacco.

A Taíno Indian artifact carved in native wood.

The Taíno religion focused upon the worship of deities called *zemis* ("SAY-mees"); this term also referred to the idols and fetishes that every Taíno carried. The supreme deities of the Taínos were Yúcahu, the lord of cassava and sea, and his mother Atabey, the goddess of fresh water and human fertility. Lesser deities included ancestral spirits and spirits in trees, rocks, and other parts of the landscape. Ancestors held great importance to the Taínos, and they traced their lineage through their mothers.

Villages averaged one to two thousand inhabitants. Houses were constructed of wood and thatch. Each village was ruled by a *cacique* ("kah-SEE-kay"), who could be either a man or a woman. The villages were organized into district chiefdoms, which were then organized into five regional chiefdoms.

The Taínos also made long sea voyages to cover widespread trade routes. They traveled in canoes constructed from the wood of the ceiba tree; their larger canoes could carry up to 150 people.

WHERE THE TAÍNOS CAME FROM

The Taínos believed that their ancestors had come from caves in a sacred mountain on Hispaniola. Anthropologists say they were actually descendants of two races of people, Central American and South American. Hispaniola was originally settled around 4000 B.C. by a race of people who moved from Mesoamerica to the islands of Cuba and Hispaniola. These people were supplanted 4,600 years later, by descendants of the South American Arawaks.

The Arawaks had migrated to the Antilles from the coast of South America sometime in the first millennium B.C., supplanting the original inhabitants of the Lesser Antilles who had also come to the islands from South America, around 2000 B.C. During these centuries of occupation in the Lesser Antilles, the Arawak culture changed, progressed, and divided. They finally succeeded in colonizing the eastern tip of Hispaniola around A.D. 200.

There they stopped for another 400 years, during which time they evolved into a new culture, and began to move west across Hispaniola and into the interior, around A.D. 600. Over the centuries, these migrants became the ancestors of the Taíno "Indians" whom Columbus encountered almost 900 years later.

"I assure Your Highness that I believe that in all the world there is no better people nor better country. They love their neighbors as themselves, and they have the sweetest talk in the world, and are gentle and always laughing."

—Christopher Columbus, 1492

Wood-and-thatch houses of the Taínos.

A caudillo ("cow-DEE-yoh") is "the man on horseback"—strong, dominant, authoritarian, and superior in the guidance of the people.

The Columbus Palace was built in Santo Domingo in 1523 by Diego Columbus, the son of the explorer.

SPANISH CONQUEST AND COLONIZATION

The promise of gold and a submissive labor force attracted adventurers from Spain seeking to obtain wealth quickly. The Taínos were forced to work as slaves in the gold and silver mines. The Spanish used the Indians mercilessly, forcing them to work long hours, abusing the women, stealing their supplies, and demanding large amounts of tribute from them. Many of the Indians committed suicide by hanging themselves or drinking poisonous cassava juice. Many more died from exposure to the European diseases, against which they had no immunity. The formerly peaceful Indians finally rebelled against the Spanish in 1495, but the revolt was crushed. By 1524 the Taínos had ceased to exist as a separate people.

THE FIRST PRIEST OF THE AMERICAS

Father Bartolomé de Las Casas was the main advocate of the natives. As the first priest to be ordained in the Americas, Las Casas started out as an adventurer and owner of native slaves. He soon passed through a spiritual crisis, however, that opened his eyes to the inhumane treatment of the natives. He spent the rest of his life exposing and speaking out about the abuses that the natives of the Americas endured at the hands of the colonists. Through his writings and public debates, he continually pressured the Spanish crown to protect them. About the treatment of the native peoples, he wrote, "Who of those born in future centuries will believe this? I myself who am writing this and saw it and know most about it can hardly believe that such is possible."

BARTOLOMÉ DE LAS CASAS

"They bear no arms, and are all naked and of no skill in arms, and so very cowardly that a thousand would not stand against three. They are fit to be ordered about and made to work, to sow and do everything else that may be needed."

—Christopher Columbus, December 16, 1492

In 1503, the colonists of Santo Domingo began to import slaves from Africa to meet the growing demand for labor in the cultivation of sugarcane. By 1520, the labor force consisted almost exclusively of African slaves.

The huge tracts of land originally granted by the Spanish crown gave the landowners virtually sovereign authority. The political culture of the *caudillo* developed, based on the paternalism, personalism, and authoritarian rule of a strong leader.

By the early 16th century, Santo Domingo's prestige had begun to decline. Santo Domingo stagnated for the next 250 years, as the Spanish crown gave its attention to the richer Mexico and Peru. The sluggishness of the 16th and 17th centuries in Santo Domingo was interrupted only on occasion by armed engagements with French and English pirates. In 1586, Sir Francis Drake captured the city of Santo Domingo and demanded a ransom from the Spanish government for its return.

SAINT DOMINGUE AND SANTO DOMINGO

Harassed by pirates, in 1697 Spain signed the Treaty of Ryswick, which ceded the western third of Hispaniola to France. France named its new colony Saint Domingue, which later became present-day Haiti.

In 1791, the slaves of Saint Domingue revolted against the white landowners under the leadership of Francois-Dominique Toussaint L'Ouverture, a former slave. In 1797, Spain surrendered the entire island to Toussaint, who freed the slaves and established a constitution. France continued to battle the revolutionaries for control of Santo Domingo until 1809, when Spanish rule was reestablished.

The era following Spain's repossession of Santo Domingo was an unhappy one for the colony. Poorly administered, the economy of Santo Domingo deteriorated severely and the colonists began to grow restless with their colonial status.

On November 30, 1821, Spain's lieutenant governor for Santo Domingo, José Nuñez de Cáceres, declared the colony independent and christened it Spanish Haiti. The new nation, insecure about its sovereignty and small size, immediately requested admission to Simon Bolívar's Republic of Gran Colombia, but before they could respond, Haitian president Jean-Pierre Boyer invaded Santo Domingo. Haiti occupied the Spanish-speaking side of Hispaniola from 1821 until 1843. It was a period of economic decline for the island and engendered lasting resentment toward Haitians.

JUAN PABLO DUARTE: FATHER OF THE REPUBLIC

Duarte, the son of a prominent Santo Domingo family, returned home in 1833, after seven years of study in Europe. He was unlike the typical Dominican *caudillo*; he was principled, an idealist, ascetic in his habits, and a genuine nationalist. In 1838, he organized a secret resistance movement called La Trinitaria, or The Trinity.

Unfortunately, Duarte was sick and out of the country when the moment of revolution arrived in 1844. When he returned to the new Dominican Republic on March 14, he was received with great adulation and celebration. Although he never held the office of president, he is considered the father of the Dominican Republic. Duarte was exiled by Santana and spent the rest of his life in Venezuela, where he died in 1876.

INDEPENDENCE

Juan Pablo Duarte and a group of co-conspirators planned a revolution that succeeded on February 27, 1844, forming the Dominican Republic. The date is now celebrated as Independence Day.

For the next 20 years General Pedro Santana Familias and General Buenaventura Báez Méndez fought for power and took turns seizing the presidency from each other. They each used their position to enrich themselves, their families, and their supporters at the public's expense.

Santana had the Dominican Republic annexed by Spain on March 17, 1861. Dominicans, however, quickly rebelled against the annexation. On March 3, 1865, the Queen of Spain repealed the annexation, prompted in part by the end of the Civil War in the United States. With its attention no longer consumed by internal conflict, the United States would surely renew its enforcement of the Monroe Doctrine, which prohibited the presence of European powers in the Western Hemisphere.

In the aftermath of Spain's departure, a power struggle ensued between the northern Cibao region and the south. From 1865 until 1882 the presidency changed hands 12 times.

Intensive development of the export sugar industry made Saint Domingue the most productive colony in the Americas, but required large numbers of slaves, who were badly treated. Since Santo Domingo imported fewer slaves and allowed them to buy their freedom cheaply, Dominican society had a much more evenly distributed population.

FROM DICTATORSHIP TO ANARCHY

The power struggles after the restoration ended with the presidency of Ulises Heureaux in 1882. In spite of a constitutional two-year term limit, he managed to maintain power until his death in 1899. His personal extravagance and the support of his secret police resulted in a mounting foreign debt that weighed heavily on the economy. Heureaux was shot on July 26, 1899, as he passed through the town of Moca.

The country was quickly plunged into renewed factionalism and economic disaster, as foreign governments called for payment on the loans taken out by Heureaux. In 1905, the U.S. government and the Dominican Republic signed a financial accord in which the United States agreed to take responsibility for repaying the country's debts, by collecting all customs duties and allocating the revenues. This lasted until 1941.

Ulises Heureaux ruled the Dominican Republic from 1882 to 1899, during which time he manipulated elections, repressed dissent, circulated destructive rumors about his political opponents, and attacked and imprisoned their supporters. He also established an extensive network of secret police, spies, and assassins.

U.S. OCCUPATION (1916–1924) Heated political rivalries continued, along with violence and instability. U.S. President Woodrow Wilson finally sent in the U.S. Marines to establish control and declared a military government in November 1916. The United States cited fears that Europe would try to intervene in the Dominican conflict, which would have been a violation of the U.S.-proclaimed Monroe Doctrine.

The Marines restored order throughout most of the country; and the military government balanced the budget, reduced the debt, resumed economic growth, and improved the infrastructure. For the first time, all the regions were linked by roads. One of the most significant changes was

that the United States replaced the old partisan military forces with a supposedly nonpartisan, professional military organization called the Dominican Constabulary Guard.

Dominicans were, however, resentful of the loss of their independence. Nor was the U.S. occupation of the island particularly popular in the United States. On June 21, 1921, President Harding proposed a plan for withdrawal. The final agreement included a requirement for the Dominicans to hold elections, a loan by the United States of $2.5 million for public works and other expenses, and acceptance of U.S. officers for the National Guard. Horacio Vásquez Lajara was elected on March 15, 1924, and the U.S. occupation ended.

The period immediately following the U.S. occupation was one of increased exports, expanded public works, and an improved economy. In 1927, however, Vásquez tried to extend his term from four to six years, thus providing the catalyst for resumed struggles between rival *caudillos*.

The U.S. occupation of the Dominican Republic completed U.S. control of the entire island of Hispaniola, since the United States had already seized control of Haiti in 1915.

By 1904 the United States was beginning to take a greater interest in the affairs of Caribbean nations, in connection with the building of the Panama Canal.

ERA OF TRUJILLO

Renewed rivalries were squelched by the election of General Rafael Leonidas Trujillo Molina in May 1930. The army ensured his election by harassing and intimidating electoral officials and eliminating potential political opponents. At his request, the "Era of Trujillo" was proclaimed by the congress at his inauguration.

Trujillo dominated Dominican politics, either directly or indirectly, for over 30 years. Many Dominicans contend that his influence is still alive today. He held office from 1930 to 1938, and again from 1942 to 1952, regardless of constitutional term limitations. In the interim years, he ruled through puppet presidents.

Under Trujillo, the quality of life improved for many Dominicans. The economy expanded, the foreign debt was eliminated, the currency remained stable, the middle class grew, and public works projects proliferated. Trujillo improved the road system, expanded the port facilities, and constructed airports and public buildings. He expanded the system of public education, which brought down the illiteracy rate.

There was a dark side to his rule, however. He maintained a highly effective secret police force that monitored and sometimes eliminated opponents both domestically and abroad. He maintained his base of support in the military by paying the officers well, giving them generous

Trujillo's massacre of 20,000 Haitians living in the Dominican Republic and his attempt to assassinate the president of Venezuela turned international, and particularly U.S., opinion against him, and eventually led to his assassination.

side benefits, expanding their forces and equipment, and controlling the officers through fear, patronage, and frequently rotated assignments. He also used the state to enrich himself by an enormous amount; by the end of his rule, the Trujillo family was the largest landowner in the Dominican Republic. His most outrageous deed was the massacre in 1937 of more than 20,000 Haitians living in the Dominican Republic in retaliation for the execution by the Haitian government of Trujillo's most valued covert agents in Haiti.

He also became increasingly paranoid about his personal safety. At one point in 1960, he tried to assassinate the Venezuelan president Rómulo Betancourt, sure that Betancourt was plotting against him.

The Organization of American States called for an end to diplomatic relations with the Dominican Republic in 1960; the United States broke relations soon after. On May 30, 1961, Trujillo was assassinated, with weapons provided by the U.S. Central Intelligence Agency.

RAFAEL TRUJILLO: *CAUDILLO EXTRAORDINARIO*

Trujillo was a product of the military constabulary created under the U.S. occupation. He was a commander who came from a humble background. He had enlisted in the National Police in 1918, when upper-class Dominicans were refusing to collaborate with the occupying forces of the United States.

Trujillo rose quickly in the officer corps, all the while building a network of allies and supporters. However much the U.S. officials wanted to see the new military as a professional and apolitical force, Trujillo knew that it was in fact the main source of power in the Republic, and that it would be his path to power.

He inspired both fear and awe in Dominicans. Because they desired peace and dreaded chaos, they admired him for the order he imposed on the society; but they feared the means by which he achieved it. He is nostalgically remembered by many Dominicans as a stern father.

After being deposed by a coup in 1963, Juan Bosch ran for president again in 1966. Balaguer won with 57% of the vote, partly because many Dominicans were afraid that voting for Bosch would incite renewed violence. Bosch has never regained the presidency.

CIVIL WAR

After a couple of brief struggles for power, Dominicans elected as president Juan Bosch Gaviño, on December 20, 1962, in the first free elections in nearly four decades. Bosch was a scholar and poet who had organized opposition to Trujillo while in exile, through the Dominican Revolutionary Party (PRD). His social and economic policies, such as land reform, demonstrated concern for the welfare of the poor.

The constitution of 1963 separated church and state, guaranteed civil and individual rights, and endorsed civilian control of the military. Powerful institutions such as the military and the Roman Catholic Church resented these restrictions and warned that the constitution was influenced by Communists and would lead to "another Cuba." The military staged a coup on September 25, 1963.

Supporters of Bosch and members of the PRD, calling themselves Constitutionalists (in reference to the 1963 constitution), launched a revolution on April 25, 1965. Conservative forces in the military, calling themselves Loyalists, retaliated the next day. The Constitutionalists refused to back down.

On April 28, the United States sent a force of 20,000 to Santo Domingo in support of the Loyalists, believing that the Constitutionalists were dominated by Communists. A provisional government was established and elections were organized for July of the following year. Meanwhile, violent skirmishes continued.

DEMOCRATIZATION: THE 1966 CONSTITUTION

The elections of July 1, 1966, between Trujillo's designated successor Joaquín Balaguer and the deposed president Juan Bosch introduced into Dominican politics a rivalry that would endure into the 1990s. Balaguer served as president for the next 12 years, one of the most economically successful periods of Dominican history, due in part to high sugar prices on the international market. In the late 1970s, however, as sugar prices fell and the price of oil increased, the Dominican economy faltered. Support for Balaguer's administration plummeted as inflation and unemployment soared.

Balaguer's military forces tried again in 1978 to manipulate the elections, but U.S. President Jimmy Carter sent a naval deployment to the Republic, pressuring them to respect the democratic process. Silvestre Antonio Guzmán Fernández, the PRD candidate, won the presidency. He combined social and economic reforms with conservative economic austerity measures to combat rising oil prices and declining sugar prices.

Although Guzmán's administration suffered from a declining external economy and severe hurricane damage in 1979, another PRD candidate, Salvador Jorge Blanco, won the presidency in 1982. A recession in the United States and Europe and the international debt crisis forced Jorge to implement unpopular austerity measures. Riots broke out in 1985.

Balaguer won back the presidency in 1986. Although nearly blind and more than 85 years old, he continues to maintain power. Economic crises have continued, however, as well as violent protests.

Balaguer followed the dictator Trujillo's example in intimidating his opponents and controlling the military. Bosch's party, the PRD, boycotted the 1970 and the 1974 elections in order to avoid attacks on its candidates. Also like Trujillo, Balaguer has used the National Police as a tool of repression.

GOVERNMENT

THE DOMINICAN REPUBLIC'S dramatic history has centered on politics. Political power almost always depends on who one knows—one's family, friends, and business associates. While formal organizations are important, the informal ties carry perhaps even greater weight.

The Dominican Republic wavers between two political traditions: authoritarianism and democracy. Dominicans admire the principles of a liberal democracy in the abstract, but they often secretly prefer the disciplined rule of a strong *caudillo*. Many Dominicans seem to fear that democracy will not work in their country. Over the decades since the end of the Trujillo dictatorship, certain democratic principles have become accepted, but many only superficially so.

ELECTORAL SYSTEM

Voting is compulsory in the Dominican Republic for all citizens 18 years or older and for any married individuals regardless of age. The requirement is not enforced, however. Members of the police or the armed forces are not allowed to vote, nor are imprisoned criminals. Ballots are color-coded to compensate for the high rate of illiteracy. Voters receive two separate ballots for each of the competing political parties. They deposit one for the presidential election and one for all other contested offices. This system in effect forces the voter to elect a single party rather than individuals to office, thus explaining why the president's party almost always carries a majority in congress.

Above: **A carload of enthusiastic voters. The Dominican Republic's current electoral system was established after Trujillo's assassination in 1961, under the recommendations given by the Organization of American States.**

CONSTITUTION OF 1966

By 1989, the country had experienced 29 constitutions in less than 150 years of independence. Emerging from the era of Trujillo, Dominicans desired a firm commitment to constitutionalism, that is, loyalty to a set of governing principles, rather than loyalty to a leader. Although the constitutionalist ideal was not popular with aspiring *caudillos*, the 1966 constitution has lasted into the 1990s with only a few amendments.

The 1966 document formed a compromise between the authoritarian history of the Dominican Republic and the ideals of democracy. While it established a lengthy list of basic rights and civil liberties and provided for a strengthened legislature, it also granted a great deal of power to the president, including emergency prerogatives that, whenever exercised, historically have preceded a state of dictatorship.

The 1966 constitution reaffirmed and strengthened several basic democratic principles that had been historically present in the Dominican Republic, but not always exercised. These basic principles included representative government by direct vote; the separation of powers into executive, legislative, and judicial branches; a system of checks and balances between the branches of government; and the right to civil and political liberties.

The constitution defines few limitations on the president's power. It requires him to obtain congressional consent to certain appointments, treaty negotiations, entry into certain contracts, and for the use of emergency powers. With the Dominican electoral system, however, the president's party almost always holds a majority in Congress; so his wishes are rarely at risk of being defeated.

EXECUTIVE POWER

The president and vice-president are elected directly to office. They are limited to a four-year term, but may run for reelection. The president appoints a cabinet of approximately 15 secretaries, and as executive, has authority over the appointment and dismissal of almost all public officials.

The Dominican Republic has a very strong executive office. The 1966 constitution gives the president the power to promulgate the laws passed by congress; to engage in diplomatic relations; as well as to command, to deploy, and to make appointments in the armed forces. His extensive emergency powers include the right to suspend basic rights in times of emergency, to postpone congressional sessions, to declare a state of siege, and to rule by decree.

PRESIDENT JOAQUÍN BALAGUER

President Joaquín Balaguer was Trujillo's puppet president at the time of the dictator's assassination. Balaguer was known as a poet, an historian, and a scholar. Small of stature and meek in manner, he nevertheless has distinguished himself as one of the shrewdest politicians in Dominican history. From Trujillo, he learned how to maneuver through the choppy waters of Dominican politics, yet he has also demonstrated that he can adapt his authoritarian tendencies to the rising democratic winds.

Although 86 years old and nearly blind, he ran for reelection in 1994. When asked what he would say to those who think that he and his main political rival, Juan Bosch, are too old to be president, he replied with a chuckle, "They are right. We are too old." Nonetheless, with the undying spirit of a Dominican *caudillo*, he won reelection.

The National Palace, built by Trujillo in 1939, still houses government offices.

LEGISLATIVE POWER

The 1966 constitution gives all legislative powers to the bicameral congress, which consists of a senate and a chamber of deputies. Members of both houses are elected directly for four-year terms, which coincide with the presidential terms. The senate has 30 members, one from each province and another from the national district government of Santo Domingo. The chamber of deputies has approximately 120 members, who are elected by a system of proportional representation from provincial districts. One representative stands for every 50,000 inhabitants of a district, providing that each district has a minimum of two deputies.

The constitution gives the congress power to levy taxes, to change the country's political subdivisions, to declare a state of emergency, to regulate immigration, to approve or to reject extraordinary expenditures requested by the executive, to legislate on all matters concerning the public debt, to examine annually all acts of the president, to interrogate cabinet ministers (although it does not confirm them for office), and to legislate on all matters not within the constitutional mandate of other branches of the government.

The 1966 constitution broadened the powers of congress considerably. The legislative branch continued in its historically weak role, however, until 1978, when full democracy was restored under Presidents Guzmán and Jorge. The congress is not yet fully independent of the executive's control, but it can check him to a limited extent.

JUDICIAL POWER

The judicial branch of government is headed by the Supreme Court of Justice, consisting of nine members. It is the ultimate court of appeal, and it decides any case involving the president, vice-president, cabinet members, congress members, or judges and prosecutors of the higher courts. The supreme court also administers the entire judicial system, including the dismissal or transfer of lower court judges.

Judges serve four-year renewable terms that coincide with presidential and congressional terms. This means that, though appointed rather than elected, they may be influenced by the prevailing political climate in the process of making their judicial decisions. Moreover, the supreme court has no power of judicial review; thus, it may not review the constitutionality of laws promulgated by either the congress or the president. In practical terms, this makes the judiciary the weakest branch of government.

The Dominican judicial system is based on the Napoleonic code, in which cases are tried according to reasoning based on what the code says, as opposed to reasoning based on historical precedent.

35

Balaguer and the PRSC won the 1994 presidential elections. José Peña Gómez from the PRD came in second and accused Balaguer and the PRSC of fraud. Bosch came in third with the PLD.

POLITICAL PARTIES

Two main parties have dominated Dominican political life since the 1960s: the Reformist Party (PR) and the Dominican Revolutionary Party (PRD). The PRD was established in 1939 by Dominican exiles opposing the Trujillo dictatorship. Juan Bosch began his political career within the left-of-center, democratically-oriented PRD, but later split and formed a more radical party, the Dominican Liberation Party (PLD). Presidents Silvestre Guzmán and Salvador Jorge were both elected through the PRD, which seeks to assist peasants and workers to implement social change.

The other major party, the PR, has served as President Balaguer's personal political machine for more than two decades. Although generally more conservative ideologically, the party has generally served more to promote patronage than to put forth a particular political platform.

In 1985, Balaguer promoted a union with the Revolutionary Social Christian Party (PRSC), forming the Social Christian Reformist Party (still designated by the initials PRSC). It gives Balaguer a more legitimate base of support through trade unions and student and campesino organizations affiliated with the International Christian Democrats.

In addition to Bosch's PLD, the two main political parties of the far left include the Dominican Communist Party (PCD) and the Socialist Bloc (SB).

THE ARMED FORCES

In spite of recognizing the importance to democracy of a professional and nonpolitical military, the armed forces continue to play a political role within the Dominican Republic, although in a more indirect manner today than earlier in the country's history. The Dominican government has actively worked to reduce the political role of the armed forces since 1978. Members of the armed forces and the police are not allowed to vote or to participate in the activities of political parties or labor unions.

The armed forces consists of the army, the navy, and the air force. The combined strength of these forces totals 20,800 members, equaling 3.3 military personnel for every 1,000 citizens, which is a lower ratio than the average Latin American country.

Though the Dominican Republic has not confronted any serious external threats for many years, it continues to perceive Haiti and Cuba as potential threats to national security. Haiti poses a concern due to internal political upheavals that could realistically bleed over the border in the form of refugees. The Dominican Republic does not fear an overt attack by Cuba, so much as it fears that Cuba will sponsor Dominican dissidents to revolt, as happened in 1959 during the Trujillo dictatorship.

The unofficial mission of the armed forces is to maintain internal security and public order within the country. Only a few underground insurgency groups still operate in the Dominican Republic, however, and they represent little threat to internal security. While the National Police are officially responsible for maintaining internal security, they often receive assistance from the armed forces. The armed forces have been summoned in the recent past, for example, to assist the police in quelling civil unrest such as strikes and protest rioting—most notably in 1984, 1985, and again in 1988 and 1990.

The constitution requires the armed forces to pursue civic action programs in addition to defense duties, and to participate in social and economic development projects such as digging wells, constructing roads, building houses and schools, providing medical and dental assistance to citizens, and protecting and replanting forests.

ECONOMY

SUGAR HAS DEFINED the Dominican economy since colonial days, but it has made the economy extremely vulnerable to external conditions. Today the Dominican Republic is actively seeking to diversify its economy by branching into mining, tourism, assembly manufacturing, and the development of industrial free-zones, many of which serve foreign companies.

In 1987, the Dominican Republic was the third poorest country in Latin America. Rapid urbanization and 30% unemployment generate a grim socioeconomic reality, while the unemployment rate in the rural areas approaches 60%. Although inflation has fallen in the 1990s, the foreign debt continues to rise.

Persistent political corruption, patronage, graft, and greed further debilitate the economy. The public sector is bloated, but few politicians are willing to cut unnecessary spending.

Opposite: **Workers are paid five pesos a day to load tomatoes.**

Left: **Manufacturing was one of the most dynamic sectors for economic growth in the 1980s.**

The Tavera and Valdesia dams have increased irrigation and opened extensive new areas to cultivation.

AGRICULTURE

Once the foundation of the Dominican economy, agriculture now comprises only about 15% of the GDP (1991). The agricultural sector employs 35% of the labor force and provides most of the food for domestic consumption. In terms of export earnings, however, agriculture has fallen to second place behind mining. The principal cash crops are sugar, coffee, and cocoa beans. Other major crops include tobacco, rice, and plantains.

About 57% of the Dominican Republic's total land area remains devoted to agriculture. The sugar industry uses the most advanced technology, but this technology does not extend to other crops. The average farmer uses little or no fertilizer and often has no access to tractors or even irrigation.

Latifundios ("lah-tee-FOON-dyos"), or large landholdings, account for only 2% of Dominican holdings, but they control 55% of the farmland. In contrast, *minifundios* ("mee-nee-FOON-dyos"), or small landholdings under 50 acres, account for 82% of agricultural holdings, but they occupy only 12% of the total farmland. Tens of thousands of *campesinos* ("kahm-peh-SEE-nohs") own no more than a few *tareas* ("tah-RAY-as"), a unit equivalent to 0.15 acres.

SUGAR Despite efforts to diversify its economy away from sugar, the Dominican Republic continues to be the fourth largest sugar producer in the world, exporting half of its sugar to the United States. Raw sugar and molasses together accounted for 21.8% of total export earnings in 1991. About 30% of the Dominican population is affected, directly or indirectly, by fluctuations in the sugar market—including some 65,000 mill workers and 40 to 50 thousand cane cutters.

Acreage devoted to the cultivation of sugar covers approximately 592,800 acres, primarily on the southern and eastern coastal plains. Three major producers control 75% of sugar production: the National Sugar Council (CEA), a government entity created in 1966 to manage properties expropriated from Trujillo; Casa Vicini, a privately-owned family operation; and Central Romana, formerly owned by the U.S. corporation Gulf and Western.

At the other end of the spectrum, thousands of independent sugarcane farmers, called *colonos* ("koh-LOH-nos"), sell their harvest directly to the sugar mills. Small to mid-sized colonos control 154,375 acres, but their individual landholdings have become fragmented through the generations as they divide their holdings among their children.

The income from sugar has dropped more than 56% since 1983. After commanding all-time high prices in 1979, sugar prices dropped in the early 1980s, due to a world recession and a 75% reduction in U.S. sugar quotas. Increasing use of corn sweeteners and beet sugar has reduced the demand for cane sugar.

Though the government-owned National Sugar Council generates 60% of Dominican sugar output, the firm operates at a financial loss and at lower productivity rates than the two major private companies.

TOBACCO First cultivated by the Taíno Indians, tobacco enjoyed a renaissance in the Dominican Republic during the 1960s, due to the introduction of new varieties and an increased market price. It peaked as an export crop in 1978, then declined in the 1980s due to disease, deteriorating prices, and inadequate marketing. Black tobacco constitutes 88% of the harvest. This "dark, air-cured, and sun-cured" variety is manufactured into cigars for export.

In 1987, $14 million worth of cigars were exported to Spain, the United States, Germany, and France. A growing number of foreign cigar companies now operate out of the Dominican Republic, taking advantage of the industrial free-zones. While their earnings do not directly contribute to the Dominican Republic, free-zone cigar companies registered sales of $26 million in 1987.

NONTRADITIONAL EXPORTS Declining prices for traditional agricultural cash crops persuaded the Dominican government during the 1980s to turn to the promotion of nontraditional agricultural exports. Successful nontraditional crops include ornamental plants, winter vegetables (vegetables not grown in the United States during the winter), citrus and tropical fruits, spices, nuts, and produce popular with the Hispanic population in the United States. The conversion to nontraditional exports was helped by the implementation of the Caribbean Basin Initiative (CBI), which provided duty-free access to the U.S. market for some 3,000 products.

Tobacco workers take a break.

FOOD CROPS As a main ingredient for the national dish of rice and beans, rice remains the most important food crop, but production still fails to fill domestic demand. After reaching a level of self-sufficiency in 1979, rice production has since fallen, forcing renewed imports.

Other major food crops include corn (which is native to the island), sorghum, plantains, beans, and assorted tubers. Dominican farmers also produce various fruits, vegetables, spices and nuts: bananas, peanuts, guavas, tamarind, passionfruit, coconuts, tomatoes, carrots, lettuce, cabbage, scallions, coriander, onions, and garlic.

LIVESTOCK The Dominican Republic produces enough livestock to remain self-sufficient and to export a considerable amount. Livestock production consists primarily of beef and dairy cattle, poultry, and swine. Cattle ranching, the basis of the economy in the mid-19th century, continues to be important. Approximately 10% of the cattle are exported to the United States.

FORESTRY The Dominican government prohibited commercial tree cutting in 1967 to counterbalance the practice of slash-and-burn agriculture and indiscriminate tree cutting. The remaining forests, which cover only 15% of the land, consist primarily of pine and hardwood. Plantation forestry provides timber products for domestic use, but the Republic still imports 30 million dollars of wood products per year. The Dominican government is working toward replacing some of the lost forest.

The government includes rice as part of the food basket given to the urban poor. Though the allowance amounts to less than five pounds per week, the government subsidy ended up resulting in a national shortage of rice and renewed imports of the staple, thus increasing the

Picking beans on a collective farm in southern Dominican Republic.

MINING

The Dominican government fueled a rapid growth in the mining sector in the 1970s when it invited foreign companies to search for minerals. Mining produced 3.2% of the GDP in 1991 and generated 47% of export earnings in 1989. It employs less than one percent of the labor force.

The primary minerals include ferronickel, bauxite, and doré, which is a gold-silver alloy. Lesser minerals include iron, limestone, copper, gypsum, mercury, salt, sulfur, marble, onyx, and travertine. Marble, onyx, and travertine are industrial minerals.

MANUFACTURING

Manufacturing accounted for almost a third of export earnings and earned 16.1% of the GDP in 1991. In 1988, manufacturing industries employed 8% of the labor force.

TRADITIONAL MANUFACTURING   Food and beverage processing makes up over 50% of traditional manufacturing activities. Manufacturing firms also produce chemicals, textiles, and nonmetallic minerals.

FREE-TRADE ZONES Free-trade zones offer companies total exemption from import duties and taxes for up to 20 years, allowing foreign manufacturers to set up businesses very cheaply. Today, there are approximately 25 free zones. Companies from the United States own two-thirds of the free-zone companies, while Dominicans own 11% of the firms, and the rest are owned by firms from Puerto Rico, Taiwan, Hong Kong, Panama, South Korea, Canada, Italy, and Liberia.

Workers in the free zones manufacture garments, electronics, footwear, jewelry, velcro, furniture, aromatics, and pharmaceuticals. Free-zone companies also provide information services such as data entry, Spanish-to-English translation, computer software development, and toll-free telephone services for Spanish speakers in the United States.

The free zones provide both benefits and disadvantages to the Dominican Republic. In addition to new jobs and the boom in information technology, the free zones generate much foreign exchange in the form of wages, rent, utilities, and supplies purchasing. Unemployment has been only slightly alleviated by the development of the free zones, however, since many of the industries employ few workers.

Stamping cosmetic boxes in a plastics factory. The free-zone manufacturing industries demonstrated the most dramatic increase in assembly labor in the world from 1980 to 1991, escalating from employment of 16,000 assembly workers in 1980 to more than 180,000 in 1991.

CONSTRUCTION

Construction accounted for 7.1% of the GDP in 1991 and employed 4.5% of the work force. The construction industry employed the majority of the unskilled labor. The government generated considerable construction activity during the 1980s through such projects as renovating the old part of Santo Domingo, constructing the Columbus Lighthouse, and creating a new suburb. After rapid growth in the 1970s and 1980s, this sector slowed in the early 1990s. The industry is generally self-sufficient since its most important materials are produced domestically.

TRANSPORTATION AND COMMUNICATION

Starting with relatively advanced transportation and communication systems dating back to the 1950s, these sectors have enjoyed steady expansion. The Dominican Republic boasts four international airports and one of the longest railway systems in the Caribbean, with 325 kilometers of rail.

The Dominican telecommunications system is the most technologically advanced in all of Latin America and the Caribbean, although telecommunications services are concentrated

in the urban areas. The telephone system represents the most impressive and technologically advanced element of the telecommunications network, including fiber-optic cables and digital switching, among other features.

ENERGY

The Dominican Republic suffers from a serious energy crisis that has retarded economic development for the last two decades. Skyrocketing petroleum prices caused the energy crisis of the 1970s; in the 1980s, the country experienced a shortage of electrical-generating capacity. Some areas experience as much as 500 hours of power outages per year and less than 50% of homes have electricity.

TOURISM

In 1984, tourism surpassed sugar as the leading earner of foreign exchange. More than 1.5 million visitors flocked to the Dominican Republic in 1990, generating $944 million in receipts, making it one of the most popular places visited in the Caribbean.

Above: **The government began promoting tourism in 1971 with the Tourist Incentive Law. The effort has paid off in many respects, but shortages of clean water, electricity, and building materials continue to interfere with the industry's success.**

Opposite: **A total of 15 seaports provide access for international and domestic trade, making shipping the leading means of international commerce.**

47

DOMINICANS

THE TWO CHARACTERISTICS that most readily define contemporary Dominican society are extremes of wealth and poverty and the consciousness of skin color. Although race divides the society to a lesser degree than do the economic extremes between rich and poor, skin color tends to be lighter among the upper classes and darker in the lower classes—a reflection of the historical correspondence of race and class. Although many Dominicans are reluctant to admit it, a common Dominican expression ruefully concedes, "We all have a little black behind the ears."

Opposite and below: **The Dominican people are renowned for their cheerful friendliness and for their spirit of perseverance.**

RACE AND CLASS

Although the Dominican Republic was Spain's oldest colony in the
Americas, it has the shallowest genealogical roots. Spaniards came to the
island seeking gold or land, but often moved on to mainland America for
economic or political reasons. Thus, not many white Dominicans can trace
their ancestry on Hispaniola for more than six generations. Historically, the
black population was more tied down by slavery and servitude, but these
same institutions also made it difficult to trace the lineage of black
Dominicans. More recently, Dominicans of all colors and classes have
migrated from the countryside to the cities and beyond, to Puerto Rico and
the U.S. mainland.

Only 16% of the Dominican population is white, or of unmixed
European ancestry. The proportion of blacks is even lower, constituting
only 11% of the population. About 73% of the population is of mixed
ancestry. The Dominican Republic has also received immigrants from
Lebanon, China, Italy, France, Japan, the United States, Haiti, and the West
Indies.

Race and Class

Although more than two-thirds of Dominican society today is mulatto, of mixed black and white ancestry, the majority of Dominicans deny African ancestry and ignore African influences in their culture. Trujillo, who was mulatto, rewrote Dominican history and racial identities in order to deny African elements in both the population and its culture. He developed a national ideology of *hispanidad* ("ees-pah-nee-DAHD"), which defined Dominicans as "the most Spanish people of America." As a result, a light-skinned Dominican will identify himself as "white," and a dark-skinned Dominican will identify himself as "Indian." Official identification cards do not mention mulattos, and the term Black is reserved for Haitians. While Dominicans like to describe themselves as *café con leche*, or "coffee with milk" in color, they attribute their color to Indian background.

The military serves as one of the few mediums of upward social and economic mobility for poor or darker Dominicans. In fact, the Dominican Republic has had more black and mulatto presidents than any other Western Hispanic nation.

Dominican society is shaped like a pyramid, in which a very small group of elites control a great deal of wealth and power, while the majority of the population lives in poverty. Socially speaking, the primary division is between the gentility—called *la gente buena* ("la HEN-tay BUAY-nah," literally good people) or *la gente culta* ("la HEN-tay KOOL-nah," refined people) and the common masses. While the masses struggle from day to day, *la gente buena* adhere to traditional Hispanic ideals of dignity, leisure, grandeur, and generosity.

The tendency to ignore African cultural roots developed primarily during the 20th century. Some intellectuals in the 1880s advocated a celebration of a mulatto culture, but such racial pride was swept away during Trujillo's rule.

UPPER CLASS

The Dominican Republic did not develop a true landowning class until the late 1800s, almost 200 years later than most Latin American countries. The primary source of social identity for the mostly white oligarchy is through kinship ties, which also provide the pool from which business partners and political allies are selected.

In Santo Domingo and Santiago, the upper class is divided into *la gente de primera* ("la HEN-tay day pree-MAY-rah," first people) and *la gente de segunda* ("la HEN-tay day say-GOON-dah," second people). *La gente de primera* includes some 100 families that constitute the cream of the upper class; they are locally referred to as the *tutumpote* ("too-toom-POH-tay"), or totem pole, implying family worship and excessive concern with ancestry. *La gente de segunda* includes descendants of the business elite that emerged around the turn of the century, and the *nuevos ricos* ("NUAY-vohs REE-kohs"), or "new rich," that developed with the rise of Trujillo. The newest elites are those who have obtained their wealth through banking, professional occupations, light industry, and tourism.

The upper class tends to concern itself with such international issues as the world market price for sugar, the fluctuations of U.S. power and investments, trade patterns, and the future of tourism. National concerns include the need for social and political order and improving the infrastructure, as well as the complex web of family ties and associated gossip.

The composition of the Dominican oligarchy continually shifted with each new political or economic wave as members of the upper class emigrated.

MIDDLE CLASS

The expansion of the sugar industry in the late 19th century broadened the ranks of the middle class to include small shopkeepers, teachers, clerical employees, and professionals. Today's middle class constitutes 30–35% of the population and is concentrated among the salaried professionals in the government and private sector. The middle sector lacks a sense of class identity, however, partly due to the fact that its members rely upon the patron-client system to move ahead rather than any common bond of social or economic interests. Moreover, those with dark skin or limited finances face limited opportunities for social mobility. While the upper-middle class is primarily white, most people in the middle class are mulattos of varying shades.

The members of the middle class like to consider themselves part of *la gente buena*, at least in spirit. To the extent that they are able, they adopt the attitudes and lifestyle espoused by the elites. Because they have no independent sources of wealth, however, they are vulnerable to the economic cycles of their country. This vulnerability reinforces the patron-client system, since they must rely on patronage rather than political action when ill winds blow.

The concerns of the middle class center on expanding their economic assets and extending their network of social and political influence. As they rise, they are in turn expected to reward their family and friends.

Small shopkeepers and salaried professionals make up most of the middle class.

53

The store owner is an important figure in small towns and rural areas.
A paternalistic relationship develops between the farmer and the store owner, in which the store owner dispenses not only credit but advice.

LOWER CLASS

The concerns of two-thirds of Dominicans center on issues of day-to-day survival. Mostly illiterate and unskilled, they struggle for food, shelter, clothing, and jobs. Indeed, a quarter of them are unemployed.

RURAL POOR Two types of *campesinos* characterize the countryside: subsistence farmers and landless *campesinos* who work as wage laborers. For every small landholder, there are 10 or 20 landless wage laborers competing for whatever jobs are available.

Most small rural neighborhoods in the Dominican Republic are very close-knit. Communities were originally settled by one or two families whose descendants developed extensive kinship ties through intermarriage and *compadrazgo* ("kom-pahd-RAHS-goh"), or godparentage. *Campesinos* usually live close to a water source in small groups of houses connected by narrow dirt paths. They depend on their close neighbors and kin for assistance, and they tend to distrust outsiders.

Approximately 84% of women contribute to the family income, and 20% of rural households are headed by women. They earn income by cultivating garden plots or raising small livestock for sale; they help tend the family fields, and many work as vendors selling everything from lottery tickets to homemade sweets. They also work during the labor-intensive phases of harvesting cotton, coffee, and tobacco; but they earn less than their male counterparts and are paid by the unit rather than on a daily basis.

URBAN POOR The urban population of the Dominican Republic grew at an annual rate of 4.7% during the 1980s. In 1981, 25% of Dominicans lived in a province other than the one in which they were born.

Campunos ("kahm-POO-nohs"), or rural-urban migrants, move to the cities seeking employment. They find instead overcrowded slums with malnourished children, no electricity, no running water, and no sewage facilities. Urban unemployment runs at 20–25% and another quarter of the urban population is underemployed, meaning that although they have jobs, they cannot earn enough to meet their needs. A large percentage of urban households are headed by women, who often earn money more consistently than men.

Small neighborhoods become the center of social life for the urban poor. As in the rest of Dominican society, close circles of neighbors and kin offer each other assistance in times of need.

Migrants maintain kinship ties with their families back in the countryside through a *cadena* ("kah-DAY-nah"), or chain, that keeps aid flowing in both directions. Kin care for businesses, family or land left behind, and assist new arrivals to the city find employment and housing.

Women, though poorly paid, earn money by taking in washing and ironing, sewing, or doing domestic work. They might also buy cheap or used items and raffle them off for a small profit, or run a sidewalk stall selling groceries or cigarettes and candy.

Dominicans' denial of African ancestry goes hand-in-hand with strong prejudices against Haitians. Trujillo's massacre of 20,000 Haitians and the encouragement of anti-Haitian sentiment was supported by his rejection of African elements in the Dominican Republic.

HAITIANS

More than 200,000 Haitians lived in the Dominican Republic in the 1980s, some 70,000 of whom were agricultural workers. Dominicans hold a deep prejudice against the Haitians that dates back to the Haitian occupation of their country. Dominican government agents, known as *buscones* ("boos-KOHN-ays"), recruit Haitians from their own country, sometimes under false pretenses, to work in the Dominican canefields under virtual slavery. Children as young as 8 years old work in the fields for 12 hours per day, seven days a week.

The *bateyes* ("bah-TAY-ays"), or caneworker settlements, have prompted protests of human rights abuses because of their often inhumane conditions. Children sleep in overcrowded bunkers made of concrete. The *bateyes* lack potable water, electricity, sewage systems, and cooking facilities. The Haitians earn less than 60% of wages paid to Dominican workers. In 1985, several Haitians were killed for protesting delayed payment on a sugar plantation.

In 1990, the government passed a law prohibiting employment of caneworkers under age 14, and mandating improved living conditions. A separate decree ordered that the *buscones* cease recruitment activities across the border, but critics charge that they continue to operate.

EMIGRANTS

Between 8% and 15% of the Dominican population lives abroad. An estimated 300,000 to 500,000 Dominicans emigrated to the United States from 1970 to 1990, constituting 4–7% of the current Dominican population. They migrate primarily to New York, where they make up the second largest Hispanic population, after Puerto Ricans.

Many Dominicans start their journey by illegally emigrating to Puerto Rico in open boats known as *yolas* ("YOH-lahs") across the dangerous currents of the 90-mile Mona Passage. They pay boat runners as much as $300–$500 dollars to obtain a spot in the cheaply made wooden boats, which average 30 feet in length and hold more than 50 people.

The majority of Dominicans migrate to the United States to escape the 30% unemployment rates in the Dominican Republic and to earn a higher income. Many also migrate in order to continue their education or to join family members who have already made the transition. Most of the emigrants come from urban areas and are better educated and more skilled than the majority of the Dominican populace.

Dominicans in the United States maintain strong ties with their families back on the island. They feel a strong sense of obligation to send money to their families. Remittances from the United States constitute a substantial part of the Dominican economy.

Angered by discrimination against African-Americans in the 1960s and 1970s, many emigrants to the United States returned to the Dominican Republic wearing Afro hairstyles and other symbols of the Black Pride movement.

LIFESTYLE

THE MAJORITY OF DOMINICANS manage to maintain an attitude of cheerful resignation in the face of extreme economic hardship. Although they may struggle for food, housing, and employment, their quality of life often depends on the extent to which they can share their burdens and resources with their extended family and friends. In the Dominican Republic, wealth only reinforces power; true power comes from a wide network of influential personal relationships. Dominicans of all classes greatly depend on their kinship ties for land, employment, child care, economic assistance, and political positions.

Although men hold most of the political and economic power, many identify the Dominican Republic as a matriarchal society typical of the Caribbean, because the women are so strong and have so much responsibility.

Opposite: **Children are often required to help with the family's work in the rural areas.**

Left: **Increasing numbers of Dominican women raise their families alone, but they are rarely rewarded for their strength and sense of responsibility. They are paid less money than men, though they are often able to find work more regularly than their husbands or partners.**

Children sleep in a hammock from their first day of life until they reach puberty, at which time they can sleep in a bed or cot.

Infant mortality rates have almost doubled since the early 1980s.

BIRTH

A particular set of customs and beliefs, affecting both mother and child, accompany the birth process, especially in the rural areas and among the lower classes. In many areas, for example, the mother must avoid eating fruit (especially bananas) while she is pregnant lest the baby be born with phlegm in its chest. She must also abstain from eating any charred or crusty food stuck to the cooking kettle, in order to prevent the placenta from adhering to "the back," or the uterus. The placenta will also adhere to the womb if anyone walks behind her after the seventh month of pregnancy. If a woman and her husband are dark in color, the pregnant woman is encouraged to drink the fistula of the Cassia plant dissolved in boiled milk, which purifies the fetus so that the child will be born "almost white."

As soon as the first labor pains are felt, the woman or the midwife takes an image of Saint Raymond and places it upside down with a candle burning in front of it. As soon as the baby is born, the saint is restored to his usual upright position, but the candle may remain burning for a while. The new mother strictly observes 40 days of confinement after her baby is born, during which time fresh air is excluded from her room as much as possible, and her ears are plugged with cotton. No one who has been exposed to the night air or the moonlight may enter her room for fear of causing her to suffer from *pasmo* ("PAHS-moh"), a term loosely applied to many illnesses, including tetanus and puerperal fever.

The mother does not nurse the baby for the first three days. She instead feeds the baby with a decoction made from dried rose petals with a drop of almond oil. Nor does she clip its fingernails until it is baptized, or the baby will grow into a thief. The umbilical cord is kept until the child turns 7 years old, at which time it is given to the child, who must cut it lengthwise with a knife, in order "to open the ways of life."

HEALTH CARE

Health conditions for the majority of Dominicans are characterized by a generally unsanitary environment, inadequate health services, and poor nutrition. Health care tends to lack national coordination and adequate management. Consequently, infectious and parasitic diseases are common. Many people in rural areas rely on home remedies and folk healers for their medical care.

Life expectancy has improved, up from a 1980 average of 62.6 years to a 1992 life expectancy level of 66 years for males and 70 years for females. On the other hand, infant mortality rates have almost doubled since the early 1980s, from 31.7 deaths per 1,000 live births in 1980, to a 1992 level of 56 deaths per 1,000 live births. The major causes of death for children under four are enteritis, diarrheal diseases, and malnutrition.

GROWING UP IN THE DOMINICAN REPUBLIC

Growing up, Dominican children often draw their playmates and friends from a large pool of cousins and siblings. Since members of the extended family often live close to one another, cousins play together as closely as brothers and sisters. In the paternalistic Dominican society, parents consider it very important to give birth to at least one son, and many discipline their sons less strictly than their daughters. Girls are closely chaperoned by the whole family, and their brothers and male cousins are expected to protect the females and their reputations.

Many children, both in the countryside and in the cities, must work to supplement the family's income. Poor children carry a great deal of responsibility and have little time for fun and games. *Campesino* girls must help their mothers cook and clean, while boys work next to their fathers in the fields.

In wealthier families, children are more closely supervised. After school they may engage in formal lessons such as art or piano, or they may play organized sports or informal games. Boys start playing baseball almost as soon as they can walk, and they join local baseball teams as young as 6 or 7 years old. As the children grow older, parents might send them to private college preparatory or high schools in the United States.

In the wealthier families, girls often celebrate their 15th birthday, or *quinciñera* ("keen-see-NYAY-rah"), with a large party. Although this custom is not as formal as in some Latin American countries, it still signifies the girl's transition to womanhood. Less common in recent years, the

In the cities, boys work long hours selling newspapers or shining shoes, while girls sell flowers, gum, and other small candies. Children, even as young as 7 or 8 years old, often work alone.

quinciñera is increasingly replaced by a social celebration at age 16, whereupon the girl makes her debut into Dominican society.

Young Dominicans love to go out at night in large groups. In the larger cities, they go to the movies together, go dancing, eat ice cream, or just spend time together gossiping, flirting, driving up and down the main avenue, and generally having a good time. Parents who are more traditional and conservative do not allow their children, especially their daughters, to go out on dates without a chaperon. Many couples, or *novios* ("NOH-byohs"), date in groups, accompanied by other friends who can act as chaperons. Young women pay a great deal of attention to their appearance, venturing forth with carefully coifed hair, decorative jewelry, slightly heavy mascara, miniskirts, and high heels. The young men slick back their hair and wear liberal doses of cologne. They flirt animatedly, while jealously guarding the behavior of their girlfriends and sisters.

Dominican males strive to look macho.

GENDER ROLES

Gender roles in the Dominican Republic tend to be defined by *machismo* ("mah-CHEEZ-moh"), or the superiority of males. Men are often concerned with conforming to a macho image. They strive to appear strong and domineering, but are rather self-conscious of how they appear when others are looking. They might try to reinforce the macho image to themselves and others by making sexual comments to passing females and by maintaining a strong camaraderie with other men. *Machismo* is also characterized by sexual prowess, so that many Dominican men carry on romantic affairs outside their marriages. Moreover, there is no shame for a man to have fathered several children— as long as he takes responsibility for them. *Machismo* also dictates that a man should be "the head of the family" and support his children, whether legitimate or not.

Women, on the other hand, are expected to be docile, protected, virtuous, and submissive. Nonetheless, increasing numbers of women work outside the home, and a large number of families are headed by women, as many fathers are absent or have limited economic assets. More and more women have also started entering politics; President Balaguer fostered their expanded participation by appointing women to serve as governors for every province in the country.

Not surprisingly, these gender roles are introduced at an early age and reinforced on a daily basis as children grow. Little boys are often allowed to run around naked (in the lower classes), and they play unsupervised in large groups of friends. When they grow up, they are expected to have premarital and extramarital sexual affairs. Girls, in contrast, are carefully groomed and dressed, closely chaperoned, and they are expected to be quiet and helpful. Most of all, they are expected to remain virtuous and virginal until marriage.

Mothers are greatly revered in the Dominican Republic, and the mother-child relationship is generally considered pure and indestructible. Mothers are openly affectionate with their children. Fathers, on the other hand, are generally more removed from daily family affairs. They are seen as authority figures to be obeyed and respected without question.

Women's roles are changing in the Dominican Republic.

MARRIAGE NAMES

Many Dominicans follow the Spanish custom of having a double surname, taking the patrimonial surname from both parents to form their own surname. A noted Dominican literary family provides a good example of the patrilineal distribution of family names. Dominican poet Nicolás Ureña de Mendoza had three names: Nicolás was his first name; Ureña was his father's surname, which he also passed on to his children; and de Mendoza was his mother's surname, which his children did not inherit. His daughter, the poetess Salomé Ureña, married journalist and politician Francisco Henríquez y Carvajal, becoming Salomé Ureña de Henríquez. Their sons, named Pedro Henríquez Ureña and Max Henríquez Ureña, became distinguished literary critics and historians.

A woman executive in Jamaica described Caribbean matriarchal society by saying, "If children are not fed, it is the fault of the man, but the fact that they are fed at all is due to the woman."

MARRIAGE AND FAMILY

The ideal Dominican marriage process involves a man asking a virtuous young woman to marry him. They have a formal engagement followed by a religious wedding in a lavishly decorated church, which concludes in an elaborate fiesta, attended by throngs of relatives and friends. In modern Dominican society this ideal, if realized at all, is generally reserved for the middle and upper classes. The frequency of free unions, or common-law marriages, demonstrates that the ideal marriage process usually involves resources that poor Dominicans cannot afford.

There are three types of long-term union in the Dominican Republic: civil, religious, and common-law marriages. Close to 80% of young people join in free unions, and approximately half of them break up while still in

Rural families tend to be more stable and the women more independent. Because marriage unites not only the bride and groom, but also their families, the husband's work is often tied to his wife's family. If he leaves his wife, he loses his source of income as well.

their 20s. Upon dissolution of a free union, the only property that the woman receives is the house, if the couple owned one. She may receive child support only if the father legally recognizes the children. Most poor Dominicans cannot afford to marry officially, especially when they are young. Many of them later marry someone in a civil or religious ceremony, however, if they have a bit more economic security.

Civil marriages performed by the state are the most common, probably because annulments are very difficult and expensive to obtain through the Roman Catholic Church. Divorce is relatively easy to obtain from the government.

Kinship ties, extended through the system of godparents, constitute a major source of political and economic power in Dominican society. Parents choose the godparents, or *compadres* ("kom-PAH-drays"), a few months prior to the birth of their expected child. Their selection depends not only upon good character and friendship but also upon the financial situation of the godparents, who are expected not only to guide the child spiritually, but to assist with its education, career, and financial needs. The *compadres* assist in paying for the baptism ceremony and celebration, and often assume financial responsibility for the child's education, medical care, marriage, and funeral. Throughout his entire life, a godson has the right to ask his *compadres* for financial aid.

The *compadres* treat their godchild with great affection, often to the extent of tolerating mischief and concealing misbehavior from the parents, especially if the child is a boy. The child in turn treats the *compadres* with a mixture of respect and affection. Between the parents and the godparents, who call each other *compadres*, there also exists a special relationship. They treat each other with extreme reverence and formality, even if they were intimate friends prior to the baptism.

While the Dominican family is being transformed by migration and urbanization, kinship ties remain extremely important. Individuals moving from the countryside or small towns to the city or to the United States depend on their family and friends to help them adapt, while they in turn try to help their family members at home by sending money back to them.

EDUCATION

Eighty-three percent of the Dominican population is literate, an increase from 74% of the population in 1986. The Secretariat of State for Education and Welfare administers the system of education, and requires that Dominican children attend school for a minimum of six years of primary education, beginning at age 7. Nonetheless, only 17% of rural schools offered all six grades in the mid-1980s. Preschool education is available in some areas, but is not required.

Secondary education is not required, and only about 45% of children attend the secondary schools, beginning at age 13. Of those, 90% of the students attend a six-year school that is geared toward university admissions. The other 10% of students who continue their education at the secondary level attend teacher training, polytechnic, or vocational schools. Many of the secondary educational programs suffer from low academic standards and high drop-out rates. Most students are required to buy their own textbooks, which dissuades many from enrolling. Many urban middle-class families send their children to private secondary schools, most of which are operated by the Roman Catholic Church.

Spanish missionaries established the Universitas Santi Dominici in Santo Domingo in 1538. Today the Catholic Church continues to play a large role in education in the Dominican Republic. In the late 1960s the Church was involved in the adult literacy program launched by the government.

There are eight universities and a total of more than 26 institutions of higher education in the Dominican Republic. Many upper-class families send their children to school in the United States.

The only public university is the Autonomous University of Santo Domingo (UASD). The UASD traces its lineage directly to the Universitas Santi Dominici, which was established by the Spanish in 1538 as the first university in the Americas. The UASD has for decades been the hub of student political activity and government opposition. Whereas the battles of the 1960s concerned human rights, students today focus on budget issues.

The leading private universities include the Catholic University Mother and Teacher (UCMM) and the Pedro Henríquez Ureña National University (UNPHU). The UCMM is administered by the Roman Catholic Church in Santiago. The UNPHU is a technical university in Santo Domingo. These private universities tend to enroll students who are wealthier and less occupied with political issues.

Agricultural workers fashion their *bohíos* from nothing more than bamboo and palm leaves; alternatively, they might build a slightly more elaborate structure with a double wall of reeds, which they fill with rubble and plaster over with mud.

HOUSING

The Dominican Republic suffers from a housing crisis. Urban development cannot keep up with the level of migration to the cities, condemning thousands of poor Dominicans to set up makeshift shelters wherever they can, in open lots or abandoned buildings. Rural housing varies from upper-class estates to the most primitive barracks for sugarcane workers.

RURAL HOUSING Many of the agricultural plantations hire large numbers of temporary workers for the harvest. The majority of these workers are provided with stark housing; they sleep in overcrowded concrete barracks with no water, electricity, or sewage facilities.

More permanent agricultural workers are often allowed to live on company land in their own small huts, called *bohíos* ("boh-EE-ohs"). In the more prosperous Cibao region, houses are built of solid palm board or

TRANSPORTATION

Overcrowded buses and vans tear through the streets of Santo Domingo, or alternatively, crawl along in its heavy traffic. Since the fares on these conveyances are relatively low, the majority of Dominicans in the city use them to go back and forth to work and to do their shopping. On special occasions, those who can afford it might take a taxi. Only about one of every 45 Dominicans owns their own car.

Santo Domingo is the hub of a transport system that carries people and goods to almost everywhere in the country. Most goods are transported by truck to the major market centers, although a government-owned railroad also carries freight through the eastern half of the Cibao, from La Vega to the port of Sánchez on Samaná Bay. In the absence of a passenger railway, people travel by bus or car within the country. The other railroads, publicly and privately owned, primarily serve the sugar industry.

The most common means of transportation in the rural and suburban parts of the Dominican Republic is the motorcycle or riding in the back of a pickup truck.

pine. The inhabitants paint the houses in unusually bright colors with vividly contrasting shutters and lintels.

The houses are usually roofed with simple materials such as sheets of zinc or tin, or they might be thatched in poorer households. Most people have packed earthen floors, although wealthier people sometimes have floors of concrete.

URBAN HOUSING Squatter settlements are rapidly spreading around the edges of the major cities. People move from smaller towns or from the countryside and establish a tenuous foothold by building a shelter out of whatever materials they can gather, such as cardboard or discarded inner tubes.

Wealthier Dominicans live in modern houses in elegant neighborhoods, often protecting their properties with security gates and high walls.

DEATH

If a person becomes seriously ill, close relatives and intimate friends congregate at the patient's house. Most of them remain there day and night until after the funeral or until the person recovers. They relieve the patient's family of all duties and responsibilities by ministering to the needs of the invalid, as well as doing the household work.

As soon as someone is pronounced dead, all receptacles that contain water must be emptied at once. Campesinos believe that the ghost bathes in every available vessel in the house, even in the drinking gourd, and they consider it "bad" to use such water. The attendants also shut or block the front door of the house for nine days, or *la novena* ("la noh-BAY-nah"), during which time one can enter the house only through the back door, even if it means tearing down a fence to get to it. Finally, the family covers all mirrors or turns them against the wall to prevent anyone seeing a reflection of the ghost's image, which would cause them to become insane.

Mourners carry flowers and crosses in a funeral procession.

The family of the deceased crowds into one room with the corpse and remains there until the funeral the next day. They place the corpse in a casket, the feet facing toward the front of the house, with two candles at each end of the casket. Close family members sit in the house with the corpse, praying, crying, and singing. They discuss all the good qualities of the deceased, recounting even the smallest good deed. The mourners, especially the women, dress in black or grey. In rural areas the mourning tends to be especially intense, often with experienced wailers who utter loud mournful cries and go into hysterical fits at the sight of the corpse. The wailing continues until the corpse is taken out of the house for the funeral.

Concrete crosses mark a cemetery in southern Dominican Republic.

Outside the house, friends and family gather in support of the mourners. The atmosphere outside is often lighter. People tell stories of the deceased, laugh, eat, tell riddles, and even play dominoes.

At the end of the ninth day of *la novena*, the mourners hold a ceremony called *la vela de muerto* ("la BAY-lah day MOOAIR-toh"), literally "the vigil for the dead." More common among the less educated people and in the smaller towns, the ceremony varies in size and style. In the more elaborate *velas de muerto*, the mourners renew their wailing, praying, and singing, and they construct a small altar surrounded by one to four candles or lanterns. On top of the altar they place a crucifix or a lithograph of a saint, a small pair of scissors to trim the candles, a small saucer in which to put the candle trimmings, a small receptacle for monetary offerings, and a glass of water for the ghost. Upon the first anniversary of the death, the family and friends commemorate the deceased with a similar ceremony.

When a young child dies, the mourners at the wake, in this instance called an angelito *("ahn-hay-LEE-toh"), sing special hymns to the accompaniment of an accordion and drums.*

RELIGION

DOMINICANS PROFESS AFFILIATION with the Roman Catholic Church, but few attend mass regularly. Religious practice tends to be rather formal, based on rote memorization, rather than spontaneous expression. In popular religious practice, Dominicans approach their God almost exclusively through an intermediary, whether an ordained priest or a folk spiritualist. Popular religious practices often differ greatly from orthodox Roman Catholicism, in that many Dominicans mix elements of Catholicism with folk spirituality.

The Dominican Republic has one archdiocese, eight dioceses, and 250 parishes with more than 500 clergy, 70% of whom belong to religious orders. With one priest for every 10,000 Catholics, this constitutes the fourth highest ratio of priests to parishioners in Latin America. The Church hierarchy tends to be orthodox in outlook and procedure, while many of the parish priests are more liberal, engaging in community development projects and developing Christian base communities. Such priests try to forge a closer bond with the people.

The Roman Catholic Church has lost much of its influence in recent decades. Understaffed and underfunded, it no longer offers its members the extensive variety of programs of the past. Although it supposedly continues to carry some political weight regarding issues such as birth control and divorce, the Dominican Republic has extremely permissive divorce laws and an official family planning program.

A small percentage of Dominicans proclaim affiliation with Protestant churches. Even fewer practice folk religions such as Voodoo, which is primarily confined to Haitian immigrants and their descendants.

Opposite: **The Santa María la Menora Cathedral is the oldest cathedral in the Americas. Queen Isabella of Spain ordered its construction in 1514. Constructed of native Dominican mahogany, the enormous cathedral with its high ceilings and immense arches was completed in 1540.**

Below: **While, as intermediaries to God, representatives of the Church may appear reserved and distant to the average Dominican, Catholic saints play an important role in the popular spiritual devotions.**

Antonio Montesinos, called the "Apostle of Puerto Rico," was a Spanish missionary. A friend of Bartolomé de Las Casas, he was constantly engaged in helping the Taínos.

HISTORICAL DEVELOPMENT OF THE CHURCH

During the first century after colonization, Dominican friars and other missionary orders were active in Santo Domingo. Not until 1564 did the Vatican establish the archdiocese of Santo Domingo and confer upon its archbishop the title of primate of the West Indies and of America. The authority of the archbishop unfortunately failed to live up to the illustriousness of his title, due to Santo Domingo's rapidly declining importance within the Spanish colonial system; nor has his stature been greatly redeemed since independence, given the country's relatively minor position in Latin America. The colonial Church nonetheless managed to maintain a certain degree of prestige through the eminence of its university, which was considered to be the most venerable theological center in Spanish America.

The Church lost a great deal of its power during the Haitian occupation. The Haitians, perceiving the Church as an instrument of colonialism and slavery, stripped it of all material assets. Even after independence, it failed to retrieve its former position. Over the next century, the Church struggled unsuccessfully to regain the right to property ownership, as concessions were granted by one government only to be withdrawn by the following government.

In 1929, only Trujillo's intervention stopped Congress from liquidating all Church property after a Supreme Court ruling that the Church had no legal existence. Trujillo used the Church as one of his many instruments of power; under his rule, the Roman Catholic Church was elevated to one point of the controlling triumvirate, which consisted of the armed forces, the oligarchy, and the Church.

In the belief that Spanish priests would be more theologically conservative and more likely to preach obedience to his rule, Trujillo persuaded the Vatican to send a large contingent of priests from Spain to the Dominican Republic. The alliance between the dictator and the Vatican was sealed with the concordat of 1954 that established Roman Catholicism as the official religion.

The Church often turned a blind eye to Trujillo's abuses of power, with a single exception in 1960 when Church officials protested the mass arrests of government opponents. This so incensed Trujillo that he ordered a campaign of harassment against the Church. Only his assassination prevented his planned imprisonment of the Dominican bishops.

Since the end of the Trujillo dictatorship, the political power of the Church has declined—primarily due to a relationship of "benign neglect" between the government and the Church.

The Roman Catholic Church was the primary agent for disseminating Spanish culture in the Americas, through missionaries and teaching.

ROMAN CATHOLICISM

With one priest for every 10,000 Catholics, the Dominican church has the fourth highest ratio of priests to parishioners in Latin America, exceeded only by Cuba, Honduras, and El Salvador.

Dominicans respect the advice of the clergy concerning religious matters, but they often reject their secular advice, assuming that the priests cannot have any understanding of nonreligious affairs. However, the parish priest is often the only person outside the kinship group in whom the Dominicans will trust and confide.

In spite of its declining political power, the Church continues to carry a major responsibility for public health care and education. The Church manages hospitals, clinics, pharmacies, orphanages, and convalescent

The bones of Columbus rested in Santa María la Menora Cathedral until the quincentenary, whereupon they were removed to the Columbus Lighthouse.

homes, as well as nursery schools, elementary and secondary schools, colleges, vocational and technical institutes, and teacher-training colleges and seminaries.

In the 1970s and 1980s, the country's bishops issued several statements calling for respect for human rights and an improved standard of living. At the parish level, some priests have tried to develop Christian base communities in order to help people to organize and work together.

PROTESTANTISM

The first Protestants came to the Dominican Republic as migrants from North America in the 1820s, and their numbers were increased with the immigration of West Indian laborers around the turn of the century. Dominican Protestantism enjoyed its greatest boom in the 1960s and 1970s, when evangelical Protestants successfully proselytized in the rural parts of the Dominican Republic. The primary evangelical groups are the Seventh Day Adventists, the Dominican Evangelical Church, and the Assemblies of God.

Evangelical Protestantism has gained a small following among Dominicans, constituting almost seven percent of the population. Although the percentage of Protestants has tripled since the 1960s, this reflects a relatively slow growth compared to other Latin American countries.

Evangelicals emphasize biblical fundamentalism, personal and familial rejuvenation, and economic entrepreneurship. Because the congregations conduct their worship services in a more egalitarian fashion than the hierarchical and ceremonious Roman Catholic Church, it is gaining widespread support among the Dominican poor. The service is relatively spontaneous, allowing anyone to talk, to sing, and to give testimony to their individual religious experience.

Tensions have been building between the Roman Catholic Church and the evangelicals in the Dominican Republic. Many evangelicals blame the concordat with the Vatican for marginalizing their churches and ministers, because it grants privileges to the Catholic Church that are not accorded to the evangelicals.

FOLK BELIEFS

Many Dominicans perceive good or bad omens in various occurrences of daily life:

- The cooing of wild doves near a house means that someone will die soon in that neighborhood.
- If an owl screeches near a house, or if it alights on the roof, it announces the death of some member of the family.
- If all the hens cackle together, a death will occur in the home or in the neighbor's family.
- To spill the oil when filling a lamp announces misfortune for the one who spills it.
- If a person sleeps with his feet toward the front of the house, he will die.
- To dream of excrement indicates that money will be received.
- If the palm of the right hand itches, money will be received. If the palm of the left hand itches, some forgotten debt will have to be paid; or one will lose money.
- To open an umbrella inside the house causes misfortune.
- To sweep the house at night brings misfortune.
- At night, when a horse tires after covering a relatively short distance, it is a sign that a ghost has been riding behind the rider. One should stop as soon as one realizes what is happening, or the ghost will give the person the sickness from which he died. To drive the ghost away, the saddle should be reversed, placing its front toward the tail of the horse.

FOLK RELIGION

Approximately one million Dominicans of Haitian descent continue to speak Creole French and to celebrate their ancestral Voodoo ceremonies. In the Dominican Republic believers in Voodoo generally practice their religion in secret, because the Dominican government and the general population deride it as pagan and African.

While the Dominicans claim that only Haitians practice Voodoo, many of them nonetheless believe in the magical powers of Voodoo.

FOLK REMEDIES Many Dominicans seek advice from *curanderos* ("cur-ahn-DAY-rohs"), or healers, and *brujos* ("BREW-hos"), or witch doctors. A *curandero* will often consult the saints to ascertain which herbs, roots, and various home cures to employ in their healing arts. The powers of the *brujo* are slightly more dramatic, since he can drive out possessive spirits that sometimes seize an individual. Dominicans consider *brujos* and *curanderos* to be intermediaries to God as much as priests and saints are.

Some Dominicans also utilize certain prayers almost as incantations. Among the *campesinos* and the urban lower class, people recite specific prayers—generally to Jesus, the Virgin Mary, or a saint—in supplication for protection from evil, or sometimes as recipes to cure specific diseases. A person might know one or two such prayers, which he or she considers to be very powerful. A commonly known prayer called "Prayer of the Shroud of Our Lord Jesus Christ" is considered very powerful against evil spirits, or against failure in any undertaking. Many Dominicans carry a copy of it as an amulet.

Incantations with healing powers are called *ensalmos* ("ehn-SAL-mohs") Folk healers repeat certain formulas for the cure of specific maladies. If, for instance, a woman faints, someone whispers in her ear, "Remember that God is, that His Son is, and that the Holy Spirit is."

Voodoo combines African and Catholic elements.

81

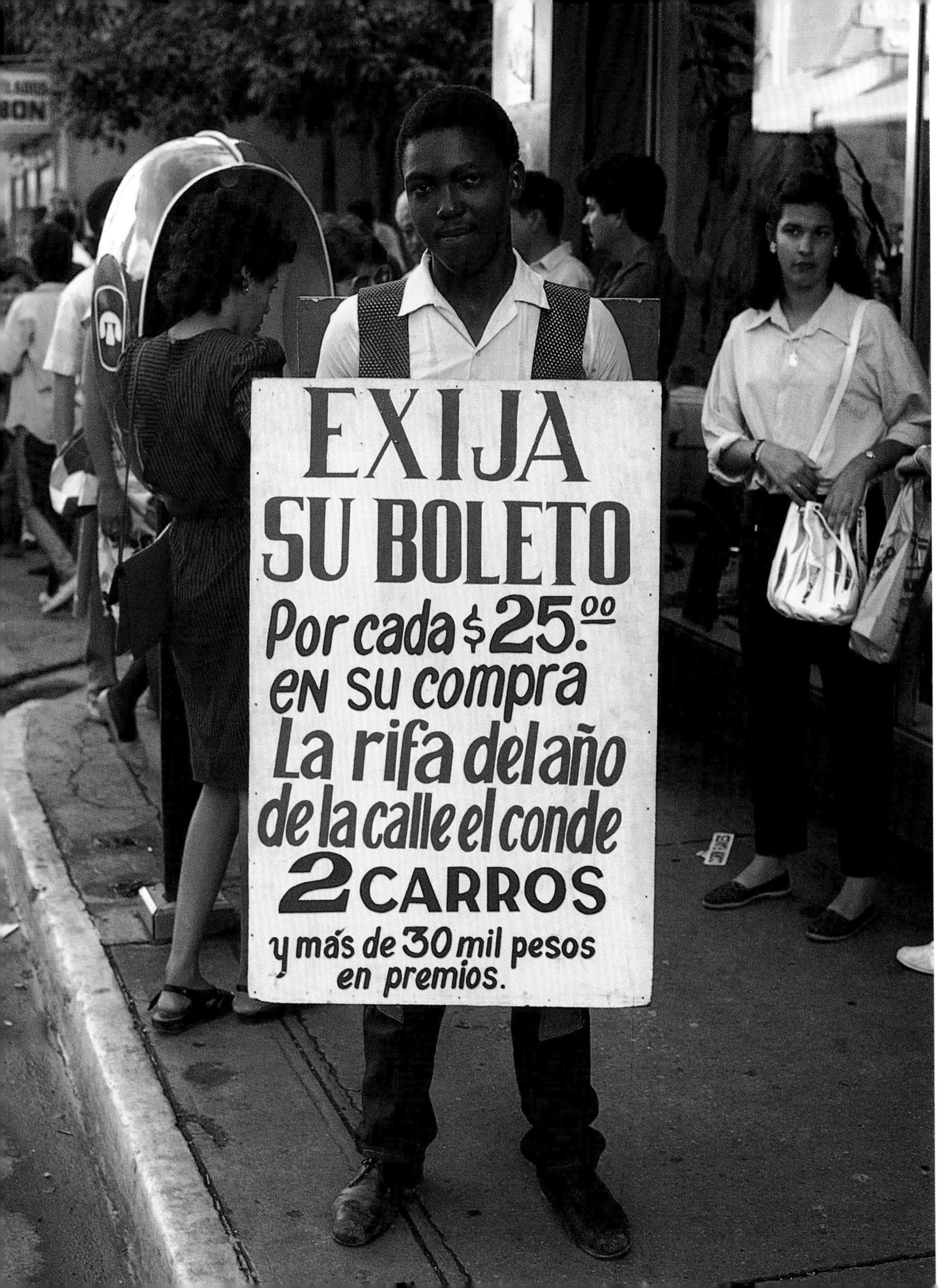
EXIJA
SU BOLETO
Por cada $25.oo
en su compra
La rifa del año
de la calle el conde
2 CARROS
y más de 30 mil pesos
en premios.

LANGUAGE

THE OVERWHELMING MAJORITY of Dominicans speak Spanish, the official language of the Dominican Republic. As inhabitants of the first Spanish colony in the Americas, Dominicans pride themselves on speaking a very clear, almost classical Spanish, just as they pride themselves on having the purest Spanish traditions in all of Latin America.

Dominican Spanish closely resembles the Castilian Spanish spoken in most of Spain. Differences in pronunciation derive from differences in the way the language has separately evolved on either side of the Atlantic since colonial times. For example, whereas the soft *c* sound and the *z* are pronounced as a soft *th* (as in *th*ink) in most of contemporary Spain, Dominicans pronounce the soft *c* and the *z* as an *s*.

English has influenced the Dominican language to a certain degree, primarily through the preponderance of Dominicans who have family members and friends in the United States. Dominicans living in the United States, especially the so-called Dom-Yorks in New York City, take pride in their bilingual abilities and in their knowledge of U.S. culture.

TAÍNO INFLUENCES

Taíno words were adopted by the Spanish to describe objects unfamiliar to them. Many of these words were translated into English, which testifies to the impact of Taíno products on a marveling Europe. English words such as hammock, cassava, tobacco, potato, hurricane, and canoe derive from the classical Spanish phonetic spellings of Taíno words *hamaca, cazabe, tabaco, patata, huracán,* and *canoa* ("AH-mah-kah, KAH-sah-bay, tah-BAH-koh, pah-TAH-tah, uhr-ah-KAHN, kahn-OH-ah"). The Spanish also adopted certain Taíno geographical names, such as Cibao, meaning "plain," or Baní, meaning "abundance of water." The city Higüey was named for one of the five Taíno regional groups in the southeast.

As in most of Latin America, Dominicans greet each other with a kiss on the cheek. Women kiss each other in greeting, as do men and women. Men, however, greet each other with a handshake, unless they are very close—in which case they might hug each other heartily. Young people, influenced by U.S. culture, often greet each other by clasping each other's hands in a fisted handshake.

Opposite: **This man in Santo Domingo is carrying an advertisement for a raffle.**

83

THE CURSE OF COLUMBUS

In spite of the fact that Christopher Columbus is considered a national hero, Dominicans have for centuries considered the utterance of his name to be bad luck. Instead of actually speaking his name, many Dominicans insist on referring to him indirectly as "the Admiral" or "the Discoverer." One commits a *fucú* ("foo-KU") or invites bad luck, by calling him by name. To mention his name is to use it as an all-purpose expletive. Dominicans exclaim "¡*Colón!*" (Columbus's Spanish name) much in the same fashion that they might cry out, "¡*Ay, Dios!*" or "¡*Mierda!*"

Propaganda for the quincentenary, or 500-year celebration of Columbus's arrival in the Americas, tried with limited success to drown out the superstition regarding the explorer's name. When the Columbus Lighthouse was finally turned on, many Dominicans prayed that they would not be cursed; even some government officials superstitiously refused to attend the inauguration of the lighthouse.

They claim that the *fucú* has already cursed several aspects of the lighthouse construction, including a 1937 crash of three planes named for his ships the Niña, the Pinta, and the Santa María, which were participating in a fundraising flight for the lighthouse. In 1946, at a ceremony marking the 450th anniversary of Santo Domingo's founding, an earthquake struck when they opened Columbus's urn. In the 1940s, a politician was pricked by a medal as he was awarded with the Order of Columbus; he died when the wound became infected. These are a few of the many bizarre incidents that have served to convince Dominicans of all classes that the *fucú* is legitimate.

AFRICAN INFLUENCES

One of the oldest and most pervasive elements of Dominican culture is the concept of the *fucú* or *fukú*. African slaves brought the word with them to the island, although its exact origin in Africa is unknown.

A *fucú* is something of ill omen that is likely to bring bad luck; it can also describe something of doom in a person, a place, or an event. At the materialization of a *fucú* in any form, Dominicans will form a cross in the air with their index fingers and exclaim "*zafa!*" ("SAH-fah")—a verbal remedy to any curse the *fucú* might inflict upon them. The word *zafa* was also introduced by African slaves.

RIDDLES

Although declining in frequency, riddling still constitutes an enjoyable pastime in the smaller towns and rural areas of the Dominican Republic. When *campesinos* gather together for wakes, weddings, or other social occasions, they sometimes start telling riddles after exhausting the various topics of conversation. Someone starts the process by offering the first riddle to the group, in a playfully challenging attitude. The group responds with a great deal of comment and criticism before answering or, if it is a new riddle unknown to them, perhaps giving up. After the answer is given, everyone comments on it again and jokes about it in light of its interpretation. Then someone else follows up with perhaps another riddle with the same answer, or with a new and different riddle.

In spite of attempts by the government and the military to intimidate it, the communications media in the Dominican Republic remains one of the freest of those in all Latin America.

The content of many of the riddles concern everyday objects, such as avocados, honey bees, needles, or garlic. Some riddles suggest sexual concepts either obliquely or overtly. Riddles that merely suggest sexual concepts but then give inoffensive answers may be recited in front of women, but it is considered improper for women to recite them.

The riddle is distinguished by how eloquently the speaker poses it, so that it works not only as a puzzle to be solved, but also so that it has artistic merit. Sometimes the riddles are offered in poetic verse.

Riddle: *White I leave my house.* *Green was my birth.* *With the maturation of time* *White I return to my house.* Answer: Garlic	Riddle: *The one who makes it does not use it.* *The one who uses it does not see it.* *The one who sees it does not desire it* *no matter how pretty it may be.* Answer: A coffin

Bartering is a natural part of life among neighbors, and they like nothing more than negotiating a good deal.

DICHOS: DOMINICAN SAYINGS AND EXPRESSIONS

Dominicans demonstrate their renowned friendliness with a gracious welcome to anyone who enters their home. Visitors are greeted with the traditional expression: *Mi casa, su casa* ("mee kah-sah, soo kah-sah")— meaning, "My house is your house."

Several *dichos* ("DEE-chohs") describe the relation of skin color to class and political power, such as "Money whitens," and "Colonels are never black," no matter how dark their skin. Another says, "A rich Black is a mulatto, a rich mulatto is a white man." Dominicans also make light of their color-consciousness, however, with the saying, "We all have a little black behind the ears."

Some Dominican sayings derive from a Spanish heritage. "No Moors (*moros*—"MOH-rohs") on the coast," for instance, means that figuratively, "the coast is clear." The expression refers to the centuries-long war between medieval Spain and the Islamic Moors, and it also suggests the

Dominican resentment of Haiti's occupation in the 19th century. Another Spanish saying that is also common in the Dominican Republic is "the Devil is wise more because he is old than because he is the Devil," signifying that wisdom comes with age or experience.

Certain proverbs and sayings carry the flavor of their rural origins. "While the dog is skinniest, he has the most fleas" signifies that misfortune continues to plague the person who is already suffering. Another folk saying, "One can always find a hair in the *sancocho*" ("san-KOH-choh," stew), means that "good things are never perfect." The pragmatic nature of the Dominican *campesino* is demonstrated by the proverb, "Better to

Even illiterate campesinos *use the term* moros, *though without knowing what a Moor is, in reference to one who is unbaptized.*

BASIC DOMINICAN PRONUNCIATION

a	*a* as in cart		*j*	*h* as in hat
e	*e* as in they or *a* as in day		*l*	*l* as in ball
i	*ee* as in meet		*ll*	*y as in yes*
o	*o* as in note		*m*	*m* as in map
u	*oo* as in boot or *u* as in flute		*n*	*n* as in noon
y	*ee* as in meet or *j* as in jar		*ñ*	*ny* as in canyon
b	*b* as in boy		*p*	*p* as in purse
c	*k* as in kind; or *s* as in sit when before		*q*	*k* as in kind
	e or i		*r*	rolled, especially when at the beginning
ch	*ch* as in child			of a word
d	*d* as in dog; or resembles *th* as in they		*rr*	strongly rolled
	when at the end of a word		*s*	*s* as in sit
f	*f* as in off		*t*	*t* as in tilt
g	*g* as in go; or, when before e or i, a		*v*	*b* as in boy
	guttural *ch* as in the Scottish word		*x*	*x* as in exit
	loch		*z*	*s* as in sit
h	silent			

ARTS

ALTHOUGH DOMINICANS PRIZE artistic endeavors of all kinds, their country is globally recognized for its music and dance more than any other art form. The Dominicans themselves seem to live and breathe the *merengue* ("may-RAIN-guay") music and dance they created. Originally a rural folk dance and later a ballroom dance, the *merengue* is danced with a limping step, the weight always on the same foot. It was said to have been first performed by a crippled general whose fellow guests respectfully imitated his every move as he dragged his lame right leg across the floor. Both the music and the dance are extremely popular throughout Latin America and with Hispanics in the United States.

The Dominican Republic also has a relatively strong literary tradition, although it is not as widely recognized outside the country. The literary arts, not surprisingly, are dominated by writers from powerful Dominican families, many of whom combined their literary skills with political careers.

With the Taino influence obliterated, Dominican arts developed out of the Hispanic and African origins of the Dominican people. The Hispanic influence dominates the literary arts, while the African influence is most evident in Dominican music, especially popular music.

Opposite: **Machine-like figures grace a mural on a university building.**

Below: **Brightly colored folk paintings for sale.**

89

LITERARY ARTS

The most significant writer of the colonial period was Bartolomé de Las Casas. Las Casas recorded the early history of the Caribbean area in his *Historia de las Indias*, which remains one of the most important historical records of the Spanish conquest of the Americas and the indigenous peoples of the Caribbean.

Dominican literature developed during the Romantic period in France, whose influence persisted in the Dominican Republic through the 19th century. The outstanding work of this period was the classic Dominican novel *Enriquillo*, published in 1882, by Manuel de Jesús Galván (1834–1910). Exemplifying the Romantic period's ideal of the "noble savage," *Enriquillo* stands out as a masterpiece of Spanish-American literature. In 1954, Robert Graves translated the novel into English under the title *The Cross and the Sword*.

A leading contemporary of Galván was Salomé Ureña de Henríquez (1850–1896), a schoolteacher who wrote poetry filled with patriotic fervor about political themes of the day. Much of her poetry was intensely personal in style.

The evolution from romanticism to

realism, and then to modernism, took only a decade in the Dominican Republic. Gastón Fernando Deligne (1861–1912) led the modernist movement. Inspired by Nicaragua's Rubén Darío, Deligne aspired to modernist symbolism—declaring that "to write poetry is to turn ideas into images."

Another literary movement of the early 20th century was *postumismo* ("pohs-too-MEES-moh"), which attempted to establish a new style of poetry and prose by casting off Spanish and early Dominican influences. Domingo Moreno Jimenes (1894–?) exemplifies *postumismo* in his work *Palabras en el Agua,* or "Words on Water." The poetry presents images floating and jostling each other in the current of incessant change.

A recent literary movement, *poesía de sopresa* ("poh-AYS-EEYA day soh-PRAY-sah"), or "surprise poetry," has developed out of the *postumismo* movement. *Poesía de sopresa* utilizes imagery deliberately chosen for its shock effect. Héctor Incháustegui Cabral (1912–1979) led the *poesía de sopresa* movement with works such as *El Miedo en un Puñado de Polvo* (1964). This dramatic trilogy in verse draws its themes from Greek tragedy and in style resembles T.S. Eliot.

Former president Juan Bosch is also known for several novels and short stories, the best of which are collected in two volumes of short stories, *Cuentos Escritos en el Exilio* and *Más Cuentos Escritos en el Exilio.* He has also written several political polemics, as well as a history of his aborted presidency, *Crisis of Democracy of America in the Dominican Republic.*

Contemporary poet and novelist Julia Alvarez writes about modern life for the large group of "Dom-Yorks" who live between two cultures, U.S. and Dominican. In *How the García Girls Lost their Accents* (1991), she describes the emigrant experience for a Dominican family forced to flee from the Trujillo dictatorship in 1960.

Enriquillo is named for one of the last Taino caciques, Enrique, who had been educated and brought up as a Christian by the Spanish, but rebelled in 1533 after being enslaved with his wife. He escaped with a few hundred remaining Taínos to the Sierra de Bahoruco, and finally surrendered to the Spanish forces on an island in the middle of the salt lake that still bears his name.

Traditional dances are relived at festival time.

MUSIC

The most famous kind of Dominican music and dance is the *merengue*, which combines the Spanish *pasodoble* ("pah-sah-DOHB-lay," two-step) and the African tom-tom. Couples dance, in casual or traditional dress, with limping steps to rhythmic lyrics that comment on love, politics, destiny, or even illegal emigration to the United States.

Campesinos from the Cibao developed *merengue* and turned it into a national obsession. In the city, *merengue* music gushes from taxis, bars, restaurants, self-service stores, and even from McDonald's. *Merengue* serves as the background music for everyday Dominican life; in the evening it turns the waterfront of Santo Domingo into an open-air gala, warmly pulsating with noise, music, people, lights, and cars. A special *merengue* festival takes place in Santo Domingo in the last week of July. All along the waterfront, Dominicans and thousands of tourists from Puerto Rico and Western Europe celebrate *merengue* with all-night partying.

It is an oversimplified, but largely accurate, description of Caribbean music to say that merengue "marries" an African rhythm to a European melody.

The guitar is probably the most popular instrument. In some rural areas, musicians also commonly play flutes and homemade *marimbas*. *Merengue* is played on locally-made percussion instruments like the *tambora* ("tahm-BOH-rah") or the *guiro* ("goo-EER-oh"), although high-tech synthesizers are sometimes used instead. By rubbing the *guiro* with a shell or with wire, the musician produces the rasping noise behind the *merengue* rhythm.

Spanish bolero music and dance are quite popular in the Dominican Republic, as is *salsa* music. If *merengue* expresses the natural vivacity of the Dominicans, their pathos is expressed through mournfully romantic *bachata* ("bah-chah-tah") ballads. Young Dominicans also enjoy reggae music and other modern African-American music, as well as rock music.

Certain regions have preserved folkloric dances which are more heavily European in style. In the south, for instance, the *mangulina* ("mahn-goo-LEE-nah") is commemorated at the patron saints' day festivals, as is *la jacana* ("la ha-KAH-nah") in the north. These types of ceremonial dances, derived from Spanish and Taíno origins, form part of the Dominican Republic's folkloric tradition but are not part of the contemporary culture. Another type of music derived from Spain, which has been preserved in the northern region, are ancient vocal choruses known as *salves* ("SAHL-vays") and *tonadas* ("toh-NAH-dahs").

The guitar is widely used in Dominican music.

The most renowned Dominican performers live primarily in the Dominican Republic or New York. Even those living in the United States travel back and forth to the island quite

Dominican composers traditionally lacked established orchestras until Trujillo created the National Conservatory of Music and Speech in 1941. Dominican composers contributed 20 important musical works that year.

93

MUSIC AS A PART OF EVERYDAY LIFE

As with most Caribbean forms of live music and dance performances, *merengue* depends upon collective participation. There is no division between active performers and a passive audience. While certain gifted instrumentalists or singers might dominate certain segments of the performance, members of the audience are expected to participate by clapping, offering encouragement, or even dancing themselves. In fact, the more enthusiastically the audience participates, the more successful the performance becomes. The exchange develops into a circular process, in which the leading musicians and singers are spurred on to greater degrees of musical execution by higher and higher levels of audience participation.

Merengue lyrics are noted for their use of social commentary on love and politics. They are often ironic, humorous, or critical, skillfully using sexual double entendres and provocative allusions. Others comment on issues of everyday life.

A contemporary *merengue* song says:
Puerto Rico queda cerca, pero móntate en avión
y si consigues la visa, no hay problema en Inmigración;
Pero no te vayas en yola, no te llenes de ilusiones
porque en el Canal de la Mona, te comen los tiburones.

Puerto Rico is close by, but get yourself on a plane,
and if you can get a visa, no problem in immigration.
But don't you go by yola, don't let your dreams delude you,
Because in the Mona Passage, the sharks will surely eat you.

—Wilfredo Vargas, Karen Records

PAINTING

Painters in the Dominican Republic have not developed a uniquely Dominican style, although the country has produced many fine painters. Several have achieved notice in Europe and the United States, including Guillo Pérez, Gilberto Hernández Ortega, Ada Balcácer, and Abelardo Urdaneta. While they portray common Dominican themes, they generally do not share a distinctly Dominican mode of expression.

The most prominent current of Dominican painting during the 20th century has been *costumbrismo* ("kohs-toom-BREES-moh"), which portrays Dominican customs and themes. Abelardo Urdaneta was a precursor of *costumbrismo*, while Guillo Pérez and Yorgi Morel have continued to develop the current within a realistic style. Guillo Pérez, for example, was famous for portraying sugarcane fields and oxen driven along rutted wagon trails. Later in his career, and in keeping with his reputation for masterful use of color, he concentrated on depicting roosters.

The more recent current of *costumbrismo* has been manifested in the work of Candido Bidó. Rather than adhering to the traditional realism of *costumbrismo*, Bidó's almost cubist style shows the influence of modern realism.

The bright colors and expressionistic style of Haitian paintings contrast with Dominican style.

Altos de Chavón, the 16th century style artists' colony that was constructed near La Romana in 1978, houses ceramic, serigraphy, and loom weaving shops. The constant turnover of foreign artists and artisans at Altos de Chavón has inspired a more experimental style of decorative ceramics in the Dominican Republic.

FOLK ARTS AND CRAFTS

Dominican arts and crafts have recently experienced a resurgence throughout the country. The renewed interest is partly due to a collective search for cultural roots among modern-day Dominicans and partly due to its encouragement by the government and international development agencies, which see the crafts as a beneficial means of lowering the unemployment rate. Women artisans especially have gained prominence in the revival of traditional Dominican crafts.

Campesinos in the Cibao region carefully preserve a rich tradition of pottery for household use and as decorative art. Decorative ceramics include the production of lamp bases, vases, ashtrays, nativity scenes, decorative plates, candle holders, and dolls.

NATIONAL JEWELS

Amber and larimar have become extremely popular materials, especially in the making of jewelry. Early humans believed that amber captured the sun rays, and it has been prized for centuries for its beauty and ease of carving. Amber is the product of prehistoric trees whose sap trapped various organic materials, such as insects, lizards, and flowers. Altered by heat and pressure over millions of years, the sap became petrified, perfectly preserving its silent victims. Amber has become even more popular in the last few years due to the discovery that scientists can retrieve DNA material from the imprisoned fossils. In 1989, a piece of Dominican amber conclusively proved that mushrooms are 40 million years old, twice as old as previously believed.

The Baltic region traditionally has been the world's primary source of amber, but the Dominican Republic holds some of the largest reserves in the world (at an estimated age of 20 to 40 million years), as well as some of the most colorful specimens of the gem. Although primarily gold or brown in color, the tones of Dominican amber vary from yellow, orange, and red to green, blue, and even purple.

Found only in the Dominican Republic, larimar is a semiprecious Dominican stone that is unique because its blue tones vary from deep sky blue to blue green—the result of contact with copper and cobalt oxide during its geological formation. When the larimar deposits on the southern coast were first discovered in 1974, Dominicans believed that the stone came from the sea. In actuality, the rivers washed the stones down from the mountain tops and deposited them near the ocean to be naturally polished by the water. One of the first commercial suppliers of the gem named it after his daughter Lari and *el mar* ("ehl mahr"), the sea. Today, miners excavate the stone by hand in open pits near Sierra de Bahoruco.

Other popular crafts include palm weaving, woodcarving, leatherwork, doll-making, and jewelry-making. Weavers in various parts of the country use their local fibers, including various types of palm leaves, to make baskets, straw hats, hammock ties, and floor mats and rugs. Artisans also craft popular jewelry from amber, larimar, seashells, tortoiseshells, bone, and coral.

The community of Salcedo produces decoratively carved products from *higuero* ("ee-GOOAIR-oh," calabash), such as lacquered purses, rounded mulatto faces, fish, Spanish *maracas* ("mah-RAH-kahs"), and *guiros*—a *merengue* instrument. *Guiros* are elongated calabash gourds that the artisan dries and empties through a small hole; then he carves transverse grooves on the shell. *Maracas*, used to accompany Spanish music, are dried and hollowed gourds with small seeds inside.

LEISURE

DOMINICANS ARE AMONG the most cheerful people in the world. They face their difficulties with resignation, and overlook them in order to celebrate life, family, and friendship as best they can. Since most Dominicans work at least six days a week, they have little time for recreation. Social life in small towns centers around the central plaza, and men also gather to gossip in the bars and poolrooms; in the rural neighborhoods, or *aldeas* ("ahl-DAY-ahs"), people congregate at the *colmado* ("kohl-MAH-doh") or store.

Sunday remains the only day of leisure for most people. Farm families often come to town on Sundays to shop and to attend church. After church, people gather in the town plaza and visit with friends. The women and children usually return home early to prepare Sunday dinner, while the men stay and chat, enjoy a cockfight, or watch an important baseball or volleyball game.

Small towns are usually quiet places. If someone manages to buy a television, their neighbors will collect at their house in the evenings. Most programs are imported from Mexico, Puerto Rico, or the United States. Whether or not they find the programs interesting, people always find plenty to exclaim over in the foreign worlds portrayed—the clothes, the food, the cars, and especially the commercials.

Volleyball is popular with
the children.

SPORTS

The most popular team sports in the Dominican Republic include baseball,
soccer, volleyball, and basketball. In contrast to most of Latin America,
soccer has only a small, though active, following. Baseball is the national
passion, fueled by international competition in the Caribbean and by close
contact with North American professional teams.

In 1974, the Twelfth Central American and Caribbean Olympic Games
were held in Santo Domingo, in which approximately 4,000 athletes
participated. The Dominican government constructed facilities for a wide
variety of competitions, including a large sports palace with seating
capacity for 10,000 spectators, an Olympic-sized swimming pool, a bicycle
track, and a shooting range.

BASEBALL Among organized sports, baseball inspires more national
enthusiasm than any other. The Dominican Republic exports more

professional baseball players to the United States than any other country, and major league players from the United States often spend their winters in the Dominican Republic, playing in Dominican professional leagues. The baseball season begins after the World Series in the United States, and runs from October through January.

Dominican boys start playing baseball almost as soon as they can walk, practicing with old broomsticks and hollowed-out coconut husks for bases. They share gloves and bats between teams, but always play with the high level intensity that characterizes Dominican baseball. They concentrate on simply "throwing, hitting, running"—without coaches, uniforms, or warm-ups. Men continue to play either among themselves, or on organized amateur teams. Those who show talent can reasonably hope that they will be drafted by a professional team, either in the Caribbean, Canada, or the United States.

Although many people think that the U.S. Marines brought the game of baseball with them to the Dominican Republic, the game was in fact

Although Trujillo was not a big fan of baseball himself, he aggressively promoted the sport and Dominican participation in international competition in order to enhance his own reputation.

DOMINICAN BASEBALL PLAYERS IN THE UNITED STATES

Between 1955 and 1980, 49 Dominicans moved to North America to play professional baseball in the major leagues. During the 1980s, the number of Dominican baseball players in North America swelled to the hundreds. Among the most famous, brothers Jesús, Felipe, and Matty Alou enjoyed successful careers in the United States. Juan Marichal played for the San Francisco Giants, becoming the first Dominican in the Baseball Hall of Fame. These early successes encouraged the signing of more professional contracts for Dominican players, including Juan Samuel, who first played for the Philadelphia Phillies and most recently for the New York Mets. Other famed Dominican players include José Rijo, of the Cincinnati Reds; Tony Peña, of the Boston Red Sox; Pedro Guerrero, of the St. Louis Cardinals; and Tony Fernandez and Most Valuable Player George Bell, who both play for the Toronto Bluejays in Canada.

"If you ask any Dominican what he is proudest of, he will read you a list of ballplayers. This country doesn't have much, but we know we are the best in the world at one thing. That's not bragging, because it's true. And we plan to continue being the best in the world at it."

—*Manuel Mota, former outfielder for the Los Angeles Dodgers*

introduced by Cubans in 1891, who had learned it from American troops stationed in Cuba in the 1860s. The fact that baseball was an American game did influence its popularity, however. Starting out as an amateur sport, the game was organized professionally in the 1920s and 1930s, during which time Dominican players gained international recognition for their talent and skill. Furthermore, several legendary U.S. baseball players, including Satchel Paige, were lured away from the segregated Negro League to play for Dominican teams in the heated season of 1937.

Professional baseball declined from 1937 to 1950. The sport maintained an avid local following at the amateur level, however, bolstered by play in the sugarcane fields during the slack harvest period. Dominican baseball thus became closely identified with sugar, as the managers and owners of the plantations and refineries encouraged their employees to play as a diversion during slow times. During this period, baseball developed a distinctly Dominican flavor, characterized by a close-knit bond between the players and their passionate fans.

In the 1950s, professional baseball reemerged in the Dominican Republic, and U.S. teams began recruiting Dominican talent. Meanwhile, amateur play had matured to the extent that the professional teams could now draw from the sugar refinery teams, such as those around San Pedro de Macorís.

Cockfighting fans become passionate about the matches, primarily because of the heavy amount of gambling that surrounds them, before and during the fight.

COCKFIGHTING

Although Dominican authorities have tried to suppress interest in the brutal spectator sport of cockfighting, many men remain enthusiastic about it, especially in the rural areas. Introduced by the Spanish, it often provokes disapproving criticism from foreign visitors who charge that it is inherently cruel to the birds. Before the U.S. occupation, cockfighting was the national pastime, but it has given way to baseball.

Popularized in ancient Rome, cockfighting is an amateur sporting event in which the owners of gamecocks, or *gallos* ("GAH-yohs"), place their birds in a circular ring about 20 feet in diameter and let them fight each other, sometimes to the death. The owners breed and train their gamecocks especially for fighting, which they begin between one and two years of age. Their handlers equip the cocks with metal or bone spurs, averaging about 1.5 inches in length, to increase their ability to damage the other birds in the ring.

After placing the artificial spur over the natural spur of the gamecock, the handlers "set" their birds into the ring at the same time. The male birds, becoming infuriated at the proximity of the other bird or birds, will run and jump at them, trying to spur and wound one another in the eyes or chest. On occasion, if one of the cocks refuses to fight longer, the handler will put him breast to breast with the other bird. If he still refuses, the judge rules that the *gallo* has quit, and the fight ends.

Lapén ("lah-PAIN") *is a Spanish approximation of the French word for rabbit, although most* campesinos *do not regard the Lapén tales as animal stories. Just as slaves in the United States used to tell stories about "Brer Rabbit," the* campesinos *see Lapén and the other characters as characterizations of themselves.*

Young Dominicans enjoy *marimba* **dancing at a street party.**

URBAN NIGHTLIFE

Santo Domingo comes alive at night. The middle and upper classes dress up elegantly—women elaborately made-up in mini-skirts and high-heels, and men in ties, slicked-back hair, and cologne. They throng to the city's many restaurants, nightclubs, and casinos, where they eat, drink, and dance to *merengue* and *salsa* music until the early hours of the morning.

Since many people cannot afford to enter the expensive nightclubs, however, it is becoming increasingly common for individuals to set up their stereos and large speakers on the sidewalks of the city, providing the city with an atmosphere of cacophonous partying. In the evenings the Malecón, Santo Domingo's waterfront, is transformed into a narrow, three-mile-long street party, filled with cars, pedestrians, dancers, music, and jubilant noise.

GODFATHER DEATH

A laborer's eighth child had not been baptized because no godfather had been found. He passed over Christ and chose the devil as the godfather. The devil gave his adopted son the powers of healing through an herb. However, the devil warned his godson that if he saw the devil standing at the foot of the bed, any attempt at healing the patient would be futile.

The king fell very ill and offered the hand of his daughter, the princess, in marriage to anyone who could cure him. When the healer arrived, he was surprised to see his godfather, the devil, standing at the foot of the bed. In spite of the devil's warning, he commanded four maids to pick up the bed and turn it around; thus he healed the king and won the hand of the princess. Just before the wedding, the devil called his godson into his cave and revealed to him that the "lamp of life" showed that he was to live only a short time longer. The boy died before leaving the cave.

ORAL TRADITION

With the increasing access to television, the enjoyment of storytelling and riddling is no longer as common as in the not-too-distant past. The pastime of telling stories and riddles arises primarily in small towns or farms during social gatherings such as wakes or weddings, during the midday siesta, or on Sunday afternoons in the park or at someone's home.

A relatively large body of folktales exists in the Dominican Republic. Most of the tales are derived from European origins, but a few have African parallels. A whole set of folktales concern the adventures of Juan Bobo, while another cycle of tales involves Buquí and Lapén. In addition to Juan Bobo, Buquí, and Lapén, common folktale themes include supernatural beings and monsters, magical flights, tales of heroism, moral tales, tales of trickery, and various tales of enchantment.

Dominicans gather in the park on Sundays to talk and tell stories.

FESTIVALS

DOMINICANS ARE in general a people who love to celebrate. They love to dance, go to parties, and eat and drink heartily. Although many Dominicans take advantage of the weekends to have a good time, holidays are celebrated with special enthusiasm.

As in other countries in the region, Carnival is the high point of the year. The fact that it coincides in the Dominican Republic with Independence Day lends the holiday special significance.

Dominicans celebrate Christmas throughout the month of December, ending on Three Kings' Day on January 6. Easter may be celebrated religiously or taken as an excuse for a trip to the beach.

Opposite: **Festival time brings out traditional dancers in costumes that reflect the Spanish heritage as well as a distinctly Caribbean flavor.**

CALENDAR OF EVENTS

January 1	New Year's Eve
January 6	Three Kings' Day
January 21	Our Lady of Altagracia
January 26	Juan Pablo Duarte's Birthday
February 26–27	Carnival
February 27	Independence Day
March/April	Semana Santa (varies)
May 1	Labor Day
June 18	Corpus Christi
July	Merengue Festival
August 5	Founding of Santo Domingo
August 16	Restoration Day
September 24	Our Lady of Mercy
December 25	Christmas

THE CHRISTMAS SEASON

Dominicans celebrate Christmas throughout the entire month of December. They have parties every weekend with family, co-workers, and friends. Dominicans living in New York or elsewhere flock back to their *pueblos* (*"POOAY-blohs"*) bearing exotic gifts. Actual Christmas trees have become more common in recent years, but traditional Dominican Christmas "trees" are really branches. Dominicans might paint the branches white or green and then decorate them with miniature works of local straw or ceramic artifacts in the shape of hats, baskets, angels, and other figures.

On Christmas Eve, they enjoy a feast of roasted pig with the extended family. Catholics then attend a midnight Mass. The church is specially decorated with a *nacimiento* ("nah-see-mee-AIN-toh"), or nativity scene, with life-sized wooden images of Joseph, the Virgin Mary, and *el Niño Jesus* or Baby Jesus, surrounded by horses, sheep, cows, and shepherds. After the Mass many people return home to party until sunrise while many of the young people might go dancing. On Christmas day, *el Niño Jesus* bears gifts to more fortunate children in the Cibao region, while Santo Domingo children receive their gifts from Santa Claus.

The Christmas season concludes with the arrival of the Three Kings, on January 6. It is considered a day for the children, who sometimes receive additional holiday gifts from visiting relatives.

EASTER

Dominicans no longer celebrate Easter as religiously as in the past. Nonetheless, for religious Catholics, Semana Santa and Easter Sunday are highly ritualistic holidays. In Santo Domingo, for instance, parishioners take the wooden images of Christ from the church and march through the streets with the Christ figure at the head of the procession.

QUINCENTENARY

Dominican leaders spent more than a century planning for the 500th anniversary of Columbus's arrival in the Americas, which was celebrated on Columbus Day, October 12, 1992. The most significant part of the celebration was the Faro a Colón, or Columbus Lighthouse, the construction of which was first discussed in the mid-1800s. Ground was broken under Trujillo in April 1948. Nonetheless, the actual construction did not begin until 1986.

The design for the Columbus Lighthouse was chosen through an architectural contest in 1931, but construction began in 1986.

The monument is a long horizontal cross, a half-mile in length, with walls slanting upward to a height of 120 feet. The lighthouse throws a cross of light upward against the sky rather than outward across the sea, and when lighted, its 30 billion-candlepower beacon is visible from Puerto Rico, 150 miles to the east.

The construction of the Faro cost an estimated $70 million dollars, although the government insists that it cost only $11 million. The expense, combined with the amount of electricity needed to power the memorial, has caused a great deal of controversy and resentment among Dominicans.

Unfortunately for the organizers of the celebration, the quincentennial anniversary became the target of transatlantic controversy over the dubious legacy of Columbus. Indigenous peoples throughout the Americas protested that his "discovery" of the Americas was in reality an invasion that resulted in the destruction of whole civilizations and the continued subjugation of indigenous peoples throughout the Americas.

Many Dominicans felt that being evicted from their homes during the preparation for the quincentenary demonstrated the real power of the fucú, or curse, associated with Columbus.

Local celebrations differ in their representations of the *diablo cojuelo*. In Santo Domingo, the masks sport multiple horns and exaggerated mouth configurations ranging from thick lips to animal variations such as the duck bill or piranha jaws. In Santiago, the masks are decorated with shells or jewels and have remarkably detailed horns. In Montecristi, the headpieces represent bulls. The devils from La Vega, shown here, are the most anthropomorphic, with classically threatening or mocking expressions.

CARNIVAL AND INDEPENDENCE DAY

Carnival ("kar-nee-VAHL") originated in medieval Europe as the final celebration of feasting and merrymaking before Lent, the 40 days of fasting and penitence that precede Good Friday and Easter. Independence Day for the Dominican Republic coincides with the beginning of Lent. Carnival celebrations reach a climax on February 27, Independence Day.

African influences embellish the celebration, which resembles equivalent celebrations in Rio de Janeiro and New Orleans. Dominicans dress in a colorful array of fantastic masks and costumes, including designs of African origin. Some of the costumed carnival characters include the *diablo cojuelo* ("dee-AHB-loh kohn-HOOAY-loh"), a horned devil who lashes out at bystanders with inflated cow bladders to purge them of their sins. Anthropologists from the Museo del Hombre Dominicano in Santo Domingo have traced this folkloric devil to medieval Europe.

A parade begins in late afternoon on Independence Day, when the newly elected king and queen of the celebrations arrive on the Malecón, Santo Domingo's waterfront. They are followed by floats and outlandishly costumed marchers from various municipalities, businesses, and clubs. In addition to the *diablo cojuelo*, other carnival characters include *Roba la Gallina* ("ROH-bah la gah-YEE-nah"), who dresses as a transvestite and attracts chanting verses from the spectators. *Marimanta* ("mah-ree-MAHN-tah") is represented by twirling women dressed in white dresses with wide skirts. Around them dance *la Muerte Enjipe* ("lah MOOAIR-tay ain-HEE-pay"), men dressed in black with skeletons painted on their suits.

Hundreds of wooden stalls called *casetas ("cah-SAY-tahs")* are set up along the Malecón, selling rum, sodas, beer, sandwiches, fruit, and other snacks. Each *caseta* plays *merengue* music from its own radio. Hundreds of thousands of spectators line the Malecón during the parade, and the celebration continues all night long with dancing, singing, and partying in the street.

Street parties sometimes include a beauty pageant.

In past years, and especially during the Trujillo era, it was not uncommon for people to be killed, intentionally or otherwise, during the carnival celebrations.

111

FOOD

THE DOMINICAN DIET relies on a great deal of starch—such as rice, tubers, and plantains—in place of meat. Many Dominicans derive most of their protein from beans, a complete protein when combined with rice. Another common source of vegetable protein comes from pigeon peas, called *guandules* ("guan-DOO-lays") in the Dominican Republic, which are often substituted for beans and served with rice. Whether rich or poor, Dominicans love to eat; food forms an important part of celebrations, holidays, and any occasion where people gather together.

Above: **Beans for sale in the market. Beans are the main ingredient in Dominican cooking.**

Opposite: **Tropical fruits are plentiful in the Dominican Republic.**

ORIGINS OF CARIBBEAN CUISINE

With the colonization of the Americas came a global exchange of foods that would permanently influence cultures all over the world. Caribbean food derives from a combination of indigenous and imported crops. The colonists incorporated into their diet the native cassava, sweet potato, hot peppers, many beans, numerous kinds of fruit, and the spices annatto and allspice. From continental America, they adopted the true potato, the tomato, the peanut, the papaya, cacao, and the avocado. From Europe, they brought many green vegetables, such as onions, leeks, carrots, cabbages, asparagus, and artichokes, which flourished in the Caribbean climate. From Africa, they introduced watermelon, millet, okra, ackee, bananas, and plantains. From Oceania, they introduced the mango, taro, and breadfruit; they brought spices from Indonesia and India.

Through the centuries of exchange and adaptation, Caribbean cuisine developed its own distinctive character. Rather than percolating from the upper-class diet downward to the *campesinos*, Caribbean cuisine came from the choicest dishes of the poor to become the colorful diet of the elite.

The national dish is beans and rice, called *arroz con habichuelas* ("ahrr-OHS kohn ah-bee-choo-AY-lahs") when cooked separately or *moro* when cooked together. This is the Dominican variation of the combination, popular throughout the Caribbean, called *moros y cristianos* ("MOH-rohs ee krees-tee-AHN-ohs"), or "Arabs and Christians."

ESSENTIAL INGREDIENTS

Dominican food is distinguished as *comida criolla* ("koh-MEE-dah kree-OH-yah") or "creole food," consisting primarily of black or red beans, white rice, plantains, and occasionally meat in the form of pork, goat, or less often, beef. Dominicans like their food spicy but not excessively hot.

Plantains are popular because they are sweet, plentiful, and cheap. Although they resemble the banana, they are larger, more angular, have thicker skins, and they must be cooked before eating. Whereas the banana is high in sugar and low in starch, plantains are high in starch and low in sugar. Similar to a potato in texture, they are often sliced, fried, and served in place of french fries.

Campesinos also depend on cassava, taro, sweet potatoes, and yams. These starchy tubers are cheap and easy to grow.

A particular Dominican specialty is *sancocho*, a stew made of chicken or some other meat, cooked with cassava and plantains, seasoned with pepper, coriander, and a dash of vinegar. Another popular dish is *mondongo* ("mohn-DOHN-goh"), which is made with tripe.

Dominicans who can afford it especially like dishes made with pork or goat. Deep-fried pork or chicken skins are also popular, as are various types of sausage made from beef or pork.

Seafood is also plentiful in most parts of the country, although certain types of common fish such as red snapper and grouper are occasionally toxic. Popular

seafood dishes include shark, tuna, salmon, cod, lobster, and other shellfish. The inhabitants of Samaná like to sweeten their seafood with coconut.

BEVERAGES Dominicans drink a great deal of juice drinks, which they make from a wide variety of island fruits, including tamarindo, níspero, jauga, guanabana (soursop), pineapple, mango, guava, orange, grapefruit, and papaya. They drink plain, squeezed fruit juices prepared with ice, which is called *jugo* ("HOO-goh"), or they whisk the freshly squeezed juice together with milk and ice and call it *batido* ("bah-TEE-doh").

They also drink coffee at least three times a day with their meals. They might also buy juice or coffee from restaurants or street vendors throughout the day.

Dominicans enjoy drinking beer and rum in the evenings and on weekends. These are also the most popular alcoholic beverages during holidays or ceremonial celebrations such as weddings.

Like potatoes, plantains can be cooked in a wide variety of ways. *Tostones* ("tohs-TOHN-ays"), for example, are green plantains of varying degrees of ripeness, which are fried, pounded flat, then fried again and seasoned with garlic. *Mangu* ("MAHN-goo") is a common Dominican breakfast dish made from mashed green plantains that are then fried with onions. Poor *campesinos* often depend almost completely on plantains, which they eat boiled, with noodles and broth, instead of beans and rice.

MEALTIMES

Dominican families eat most of their meals together, unless one or both parents cannot return from work for the midday meal. The mother often serves everyone at the table, especially in large rural families where she wants to make sure that every person receives a portion. Children generally do not participate independently in the mealtimes; their mother serves them and they must clean their plates. In many urban families, however, everyone at the table serves themselves.

BREAKFAST The first meal of the day, *el desayuno* ("el day-sai-OON-oh"), usually consists of plantains or some type of boiled root, especially in the rural areas where *campesinos* need a filling breakfast to start off the day. In the cities, *el desayuno* may consist of cereal or bread with coffee and juice.

LUNCH Lunch is the largest meal of the day and is often followed by a *siesta*, or rest period. Lunch, or *el almuerzo* ("all-moo-AIR-so"), always consists of rice and beans in some form, and may include meat, or perhaps the stew *sancocho*.

Dominicans try to eat the *almuerzo* at home if possible, although many workers must instead take their lunches to work with them and do not take a *siesta*. In small towns,

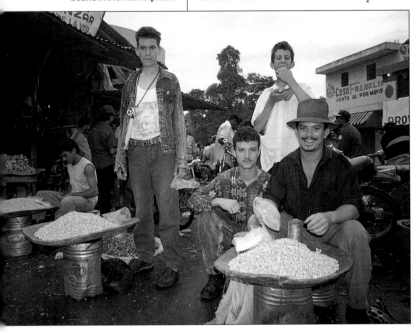

Men selling rice and beans in the marketplace.

116

all the businesses close for a few hours in the middle of the day and then open again in the afternoon and stay open later into the evening. Only a minority of businesses observe the *siesta* in the cities, however. Although government offices do not officially close, public officials are usually unavailable during the midday hours.

SUPPER The evening meal usually consists of a combination of boiled roots, with eggs, or bread, spaghetti, mashed potatoes, or perhaps *mangu*. Dominicans love sweet desserts, some of which are made from staples such as beans, plantains, and tubers. They candy sweet potatoes and red beans, and make corn puddings. They also enjoy a variety of rich cakes and the pervasive Hispanic caramel custard, flan.

EATING OUT IN SANTO DOMINGO

The country's capital offers a variety of restaurants and international cuisine. In addition to Dominican food, diners have their choice of Italian, French, Chinese, Mexican, and Argentinian cuisine, as well as a few vegetarian and fine seafood restaurants.

In the streets, vendors sell snacks of *tostones*, sausages, and *quipes* ("KEE-pays"), which are fried dumplings filled with meat or cheese. One can also buy fresh juice or sodas, and coffee or espresso.

Snacks are available from street vendors.

In rural areas cooking
facilities are sometimes
primitive.

FEASTS

While any large gathering might provide an excuse for celebration with food and drink, the most common occasions are on Christmas Eve, the New Year, Easter, Carnival, and the local patron saint's day. Celebrations usually involve specially prepared Dominican staples such as rice and beans, but might also include meat or fish, and *sancocho*.

CHRISTMAS The central dish of the Christmas meal is *lechón asado* ("lay-CHON ah-SAH-doh"), or roasted pig; the younger the pig, the more tender and flavorful it is. *Lechón asado* is served with rice cooked with green beans, and rice and beans cooked with pigeon peas. The meal might also include turkey or chicken, and cassava, spaghetti, or fresh green salad.

Traditionally, Dominican families raised the Christmas bird themselves, carefully feeding it all year in preparation for the holiday. Another traditional Christmas custom that has declined in recent years is to boil chestnuts and eat them.

RECIPE: *ARROZ CON GUANDULES*

1 cup dry pigeon peas (or substitute black-eyed peas)
2 cups coconut milk*
1 cup raw rice
1 teaspoon rubbed thyme
1 green pepper, chopped

Soak the peas overnight in 3 cups water. The next day, prepare the coconut milk as directed below. Add it to the peas and water, together with the remaining ingredients, and bring the mixture to a boil. Cover and simmer gently until tender, adding more water if necessary.

*Coconut milk (made fresh at the time of use):
1 whole coconut, or 2 cups shredded coconut
2 cups boiling water

Break the coconut and grate the meat. Then put the grated meat (or the shredded coconut) in a strainer. Place the strainer over a bowl and pour the boiling water through the coconut, catching the liquid in the bowl. Discard the coconut.

EASTER The Easter meal is based on fish, typically fresh or cured codfish, served with potatoes.

IN THE KITCHEN

As increasing numbers of women seek employment as domestic servants to escape high rates of unemployment, more and more families find it possible to hire domestic help. Many middle- and upper-class families hire at least one maid to help cook, clean, and do laundry. The maid might either live in the house or come to work only during the days.

Dominican kitchens in the cities are usually equipped with modern electric stoves and refrigerators. In contrast, since many rural areas have no electricity, mothers cook the meals in a clay oven called a *fogón* ("fo-GOHN"), which is heated with a wood fire. These women must also walk to the nearest river or stream to fetch their water, which they ration carefully throughout the day for their cooking and cleaning purposes.

The Mercado Modelo in Santo Domingo is a traditional market housed in a huge two-story structure rather than in the open air. In the front, a sugarcane vendor waits for customers.

MARKETS

There are three types of marketplaces in the Dominican Republic: the traditional open-air market with row upon row of individual vendors in their stalls or with their wares spread out on blankets; the small-town *colmados*, which sell basic supplies; and the modern supermarket with refrigerated meat and well-stocked shelves.

The Mercado Modelo in Santo Domingo is an amplified version of the traditional marketplace. Crowded with close-set stalls displaying goods of astounding abundance and variety, the market offers woodcarvings, ceramics, jewelry, tambourines, drums, leather belts and saddles, wicker, pocketbooks, cigars, sandals, mahogany rocking chairs, tape cassettes of *merengue* music, T-shirts, and even Voodoo products. Vendors along the outer edges of the market sell fresh poultry, pork and goat, as well as a variety of local produce, including cassava, plantains, corn, pineapples, passionfruit, papaya, guava, eggs, bananas, carrots, tomatoes, garlic, and potatoes.

Dominicans love to bargain over the price of their goods and become disappointed or contemptuous if denied the opportunity. The standard procedure begins when the shopper

Food is spread out on the ground in an open-air market.

asks, with feigned indifference, the price of a particular product. No matter what price the vendor quotes, the buyer expresses shocked disbelief and a sense of disappointment, then rallies with a lower offer. The vendor reacts to the offer with disgust or dismay and starts to put away the item, while simultaneously throwing out a slightly lower price than originally quoted. The buyer might either give in and pay the reduced amount, or might try to pressure the vendor to lower it even more by starting to walk away.

Small-town *colmados* sell basic supplies such as rice, oil, sugar, salt, and rum. A single vendor manages the store, and the goods are generally fixed at a certain price.

Only the larger cities and towns have modern supermarkets, where women from the middle and upper classes do their shopping. The supermarkets exemplify a more modern but impersonal convenience.

In the urban areas, women in the lower classes generally shop at the large general marketplace, with its individual vendors, for their finished products such as shoes and clothes. Wealthier women shop for clothes at more expensive, European-style boutiques.

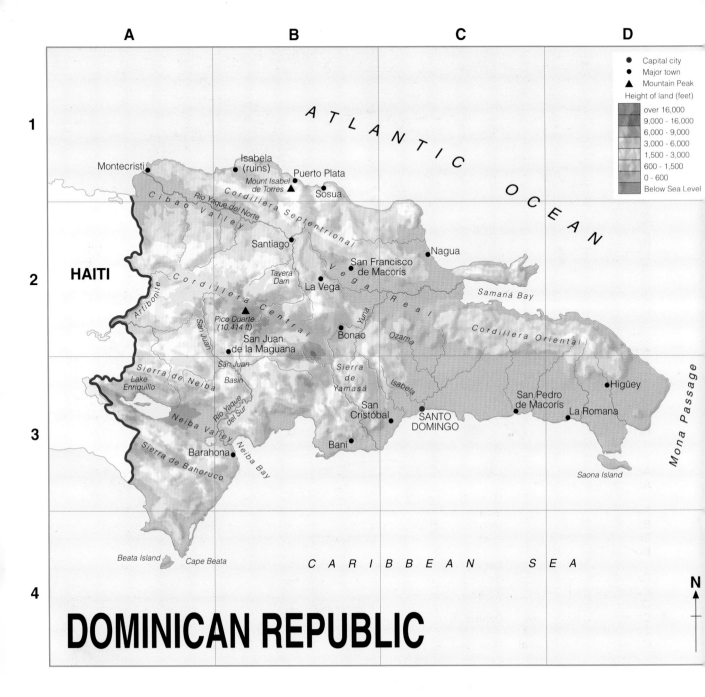

● Capital city
● Major town
▲ Mountain Peak

Height of land (feet)
over 16,000
9,000 - 16,000
6,000 - 9,000
3,000 - 6,000
1,500 - 3,000
600 - 1,500
0 - 600
Below Sea Level

1

2

3

4

A T L A N T I C   O C E A N

Montecristi

Isabela
(ruins)
Puerto Plata
Mount Isabel
de Torres ▲
Sosua

Cordillera Septentrional

Cibao Valley

Rio Yaque del Norte

Santiago

Nagua

San Francisco
de Macorís

Vega

La Vega

Tavera
Dam

HAITI

Artibonite

Cordillera Central

San Juan

Pico Duarte ▲
(10,414 ft)

San Juan
de la Maguana

San Juan
Basin

Yuna

Real

Bonao

Ozama

Cordillera Oriental

Samaná Bay

Sierra de Neiba

Lake
Enriquillo

Neiba Valley

Rio Yaque
del Sur

Sierra
de
Yamasá

Isabela

San
Cristóbal

SANTO
DOMINGO

Higüey

San Pedro
de Macorís

La Romana

Mona Passage

Neiba Bay

Barahona

Sierra de Bahoruco

Bani

Saona Island

Beata Island   Cape Beata

C A R I B B E A N   S E A

N

DOMINICAN REPUBLIC

QUICK NOTES

AREA
18,657 square miles (size of Vermont and New Hampshire combined)

POPULATION
7,515,000 (1992 estimate)

POPULATION DENSITY
401 people per square mile

CAPITAL
Santo Domingo

MAJOR CITIES
Santiago de los Caballeros, La Romana

MAJOR RIVERS
Yaque del Norte, Yaque del Sur

MAJOR LAKE
Lake Enriquillo

FLAG
Corner squares of royal blue and red on the top, and red and royal blue on the bottom, divided by a white cross

HIGHEST POINT
Pico Duarte (10,414 feet)

OFFICIAL LANGUAGE
Spanish

MAJOR RELIGION
Catholicism

CURRENCY
Peso (12.59 pesos = US$1)

MAIN EXPORTS
sugar, cocoa, coffee, tobacco

IMPORTANT ANNIVERSARIES
Juan Pablo Duarte's birthday (January 26)
Independence Day (February 27)
Founding of Santo Domingo (August 5)
Restoration Day (August 16)

LEADERS IN POLITICS
General Rafael Leonidas Trujillo Molina: dictator 1930–1961
Joaquín Balaguer Ricardo: modern *caudillo* and president 1960–1961, 1966–1978, and 1986–present
Juan Bosch Gaviño: modern *caudillo*, elected president 1962 and overthrown by military coup September 25, 1963

LEADERS IN LITERATURE
Manuel de Jesus Galván (1834–1910), *Enriquillo*, 1882
Gastón Fernando Deligne (1861–1912)
Héctor Incháustegui Cabral (1912–1979)
Juan Bosch Gaviño (b. 1908)

GLOSSARY

bateyes   ("bah-TAY-ays") Caneworker settlements, which have provoked protests of human rights abuses because of their inhumane conditions.

bohíos   ("boh-EE-ohs") Huts in which permanent agricultural workers live on company land.

cacique   ("kah-SEE-kay") Chief.

campesino   ("kahm-peh-SEE-noh") Farmer or peasant.

caudillo   ("cow-DEE-yoh") Literally, the "man on horseback," a leader who guides and commands people.

colono   ("koh-LOH-no")A small, independent sugarcane grower.

compadres   ("com-PAH-dray") Godparents.

dicho   ("DEE-choh") A saying or expression.

fucú   ("foo-KU") Something of ill omen that is likely to bring bad luck; or something in a person or a place or an event with doom about it.

infrastructure   The basic facilities of a community, such as roads, schools, power plants, and transportation and communication systems.

indigenous   Native (used in speaking of the original people of a region).

moro   ("MOH-roh") Literally refers to the Islamic Moors who occupied medieval Spain; today, Dominicans use the word to refer to one who is unbaptized.

oligarchy   The ruling class of a country in which power is held by a small group.

patronage   The distribution of political offices or other favors through sponsorship by a patron.

Voodoo   A religion practiced by Haitians living in the Dominican Republic; it combines ancestor worship, African animist beliefs, and Roman Catholic rituals.

yola   ("YOH-lah") Open boats used by Dominicans to illegally emigrate to Puerto Rico.

BIBLIOGRAPHY

Black, Jan Knippers. *The Dominican Republic: Politics and Development in an Unsovereign State.* Westview Press, Boulder, Colorado, 1986.

Haggerty, Richard A. *Dominican Republic and Haiti: Country Studies.* Federal Research Division, Library of Congress, Washington, D.C., 1991.

Haverstock, Nathan A., ed. *Dominican Republic—in Pictures.* Lerner Publications Co., Minneapolis, 1988.

Jacobs, Francine. *The Tainos: The People Who Welcomed Columbus.* Illus., Patrick Collins. G.P. Putnam's Sons, New York, 1992.

Klein, Alan. *Sugarball: the American game, the Dominican Dream.* Yale University Press, New Haven, Connecticut, 1991.

Mintz, Sidney and Sally Price. *Caribbean Contours.* Johns Hopkins Press, Ltd., Baltimore, Maryland 1985.

INDEX

INDEX

INDEX

Picture Credits